BLESSINGS OF THE TABLE

BLESSINGS OF THE TABLE

Mealtime Prayers
Throughout the Year

Brother Victor-Antoine
d'Avila-Latourrette

Liguori/Triumph
LIGUORI, MISSOURI

Imprimi Potest:
Richard Thibodeau, C.Ss.R.
Provincial, Denver Province
The Redemptorists

Published by Liguori/Triumph
An imprint of Liguori Publications
Liguori, Missouri
www.liguori.org
www.catholicbooksonline.com

Parts of the material in this book originally appeared in *Table Blessings* published by Ave Maria Press in 1994.

Library of Congress Cataloging-in-Publication Data

Blessings of the table : mealtime prayers throughout the year / [compiled by] Victor-Antoine d'Avila-Latourrette.
  p. cm.
  Rev. ed. of: Table blessings / Victor-Antoine d'Avila-Latourrette. c1994.
  ISBN 0-7648-0983-0 (pbk.)
  1. Grace at meals—Christianity. 2. Devotional calendars. I. D'Avila-Latourrette, Victor-Antoine. II. Table blessings.

BV283.G7B58 2003
242'.8—dc21   2003040116

Scripture citations are taken from the *New Revised Standard Version of the Bible*, copyright 1989 by the Division of Christian Education of the National Council of the Churches of Christ in the USA. All rights reserved. Used with permission.

Printed in the United States of America
07 06 05 04 03 5 4 3 2 1
Revised edtion 2003

To the memory of Dom Pierre Minard,

exemplary monk and humble master

of the ways of prayer.

CONTENTS

INTRODUCTION

So, whether you eat or drink, or whatever you do,
do everything for the glory of God.

1 CORINTHIANS 10:31

BLESSINGS and prayers before and after a meal are part of the earliest Christian tradition, which in turn finds its origin in the ancient Jewish ritual of pronouncing a blessing before the beginning of the meal. Throughout the centuries, Christian communities, Christian families, and individual Christians have always kept the lovely custom of reading a short passage from the Bible followed by a short prayer, usually called "grace," before sitting down to their daily meals. Unfortunately, with the increased secularization of our society, as well as the fast pace of daily life, the first thing we often put aside is the practice of offering thanks to God for his daily gifts to us.

And yet, as history has proven time and again, whenever there is a decline in a certain practice a time of revival usually follows. With the renewal of the liturgy in the last decades, interest has grown in revitalizing the practice of prayer at the table. Many do this in a spontaneous manner, but in the long run, spontaneous prayer at the table can become trivial or difficult to sustain day after day. In some parts of the world (such as Belgium, France, and Italy) the use of prayers and readings following the liturgical cycle is growing in popularity. This practice attunes the believer to the attitudes of the particular season and brings one into spiritual communion with other members of the body of Christ at large. There is a certain wisdom imparted by the Spirit when we participate in the seasons and festivals of the Church's year. We are all called to enter into the richness and saving power of the mystery of Christ. We do it concretely by prayer and by listening to the word of God, which ultimately forms Christ in each of us.

The first part of this book is a collection of prayers (with optional scriptural readings) for the table based on the daily and seasonal rhythm of the liturgy. Although mainly inspired by the Catholic tradition, it is meant to be ecumenical in character. The richness of these prayers, based as they are on liturgical texts of the East and West, as well as Christian writings derived from monastic and mystical sources show the depth and variety of prayer within the Christian tradition. It is hoped that those who pray them together in the context of a shared meal will grow gradually above denominational barriers into that unity which Christ wishes for his Church.

The second part of this book offers table prayers to suit a variety of purposes: some appropriate for children, an offering of table graces from many lands, a presentation of traditional table graces, suggestions for scriptural passages to be used as table prayers, as well as a sampler of silly graces. All these may offer options should the circumstances require a less formal, less liturgical prayer before meals.

We should remember that prayer at the table helps to bring communities, families, and friends together. It helps us keep in touch with the Lord at regular times of the day. It also helps us to remember our brothers and sisters in need. It is not proper for Christians to thank God for his blessings while forgetting the poor or those who are deprived of nourishment. As followers of Jesus, we are called on not only to pray for them but also to share with them from what the Lord has provided us.

There is something else which is well known but often forgotten—the sacred character of the dinner table. There is a profound link between prayer and the meal itself. All we have to do is recall the many episodes in the gospels when Jesus shares a meal with his disciples and friends. First and foremost is the institution of the Eucharist. Among the many other meals the Lord shared with his disciples were the "breaking of bread" at Emmaus on the evening of his Resurrection, the wedding feast of Cana, and the multiplication of the loaves and the fish where the Lord expressed his tender compassion for the hungry crowd and provided food in abundance for them. Again and again the gospel narratives relate the importance that Jesus attribute to food and friendship at the table.

A Short History of Table Graces

Grace before meals is a long-standing Christian custom that follows the example of Christ when he fed the great crowd of four thousand in Mark 8:6–7:

> He ordered the crowd to sit down on the ground; and he took the seven loaves, and after giving thanks he broke them and gave them to his disciples to distribute; and they distributed them to the crowd. They also had a few small fish; and after blessing them, he ordered that these too should be distributed.

The idea of grace before meals is greatly influenced by the fact that the Eucharist itself is a community meal with the Lord appearing in the form of food—the bread and the wine. The altar is a table, and communion is a meal shared by God's sons and daughters.

The practice of saying grace is mentioned many times in the writings of the early Church. Saint Clement of Alexandria (c. 190 A.D.) said: "It is meet before we partake of any food to bless the Maker of all things."

Tertullian, a contemporary of Clement's, shows Christians making the sign of the cross as they took their places at the table. "Our repasts," Tertullian says, "are nothing vile or immodest. We do not recline until we have prayed to God."

One of the most ancient forms of meal prayer is found in a fourth-century document attributed to Saint Athanasius. After making the sign of the cross, this prayer follows:

> We give you thanks, Our Father, for the Resurrection which you have manifest to us through Jesus, your Son; and even as this bread which is here on this table was formerly scattered abroad and has been made compact and one, so may your Church be reunited from the ends of the earth, for yours is the power and glory for ever. Amen.

The prayer said upon rising from the table is somewhat longer and more elaborate:

> The merciful and compassionate Lord has given nourishment to those who fear him. Glory be to the Father, to the Son, and to the Holy Spirit, now and forever throughout the ages. Almighty God and Our Lord Jesus Christ, whose name is above all things, we give you thanks and praise because you have given us a portion of your goods and nourishment for our bodies. We pray and beseech you to give us in like manner heavenly nourishment. Make us fear and reverence your law, and grant that we may never disobey your precepts. Write on our hearts your law and your justice. Sanctify our mind, our soul, and our body through your dear Son, Jesus Christ Our Lord, to whom with you belongs glory, dominion, honor, and adoration forever and ever. Amen.

The custom of saying grace is also found in the Rule of Saint Benedict written in the sixth century. The Benedictine Rule notes the saying of grace and the punishment for those who do not come in time for this meal prayer:

> Whoever has failed through his own negligence or fault shall be reproved the first and second time; if he does not mend his ways he shall be barred from his place at the common table, and separated from the company, take his meal alone and deprived of wine until he has given proofs of amendment.

Graces used in monasteries were long and were patterned after the offices that punctuated the monastic day. If you wish to follow this longer form, here is an example based on the *Sarum Breviary* for use before dinner on Easter day.

Leader: Bless us, O Lord,
Response: Bless us.
Leader: This is the day the Lord has made;
Response: let us rejoice and be glad in it (Psalm 118).
Leader: Glory be to the Father and to the Son, and to the Holy Spirit. As it was in the beginning, is now, and ever shall be, world without end.
Response: Amen.
Leader: Lord, have mercy.
Response: Christ, have mercy. Lord, have mercy.
Leader: Our Father, who art in heaven, hallowed be thy name. Thy kingdom come, thy will be done on earth as it is in heaven. Give us this day our daily bread and forgive us our trespasses as we forgive those who trespass against us.
Response: And lead us not into temptation but deliver us from evil. Amen.

Leader: Pray, Lord, a blessing.
Response: May the King of glory make us partakers of the
              heavenly table.
Response: Amen.
Reading: Clean out the old yeast so that you may be a new
              batch, as you really are unleavened. For our paschal
              lamb, Christ, has been sacrificed. Therefore , let us
              celebrate the festival (1 Cor 5:7–8).
Leader: And you, O Lord, have mercy on us.
Response: Thanks be to God.

In the Middle Ages, an unknown writer prepared a book of rules and duties for nuns who were solitaries. Grace was directed to be said on very many occasions:

> Between meals, who so wishes to drink, let her say: May the Son of God bless our drink. In the name of the Father, and of the Son, and of the Holy Spirit. Amen. Make the sign of the cross, and finally say: Our help is in the name of the Lord, who made heaven and earth. The name of the Lord be blessed, now and forever. Let us bless the Lord. Thanks be to God.

One meal custom at court was to place the priest at a place next to the King so that he might bless the food. In fact, on the Bayeaux Tapestry of the eleventh century is an illustration of the dinner that took place after William, Duke of Normandy, had landed on the shores of England. It shows Bishop Odo blessing the cake and the cup.

Satirist Charles Lamb, an eighteenth-century essayist, said that he was "disposed to say grace upon twenty other occasions in the course of the day" besides his dinner—when setting out for a walk, during a midnight ramble, enjoying an encounter with friends, or having solved a problem.

Calling graces "the sweet preluding strains to the banquets of angels and children," he most approved of those blessings said at a poor family's table or before the simple repast of children.

Lamb also reported that his old school chum, a clergyman, was often asked to say grace. He would say, "Is there no clergyman here?" significantly adding, "Thank God," fearing that the blessing would be overlong.

Humorist Stephen Leacock once wrote a story about a future-tense Christmas dinner, where dinner was reduced to the pill. Only the addition of water was needed to reconstitute the meal. He described a large traditional family gathering assembled at the table, saying grace over a single pill that contained a veritable feast of turkey, stuffing, cranberry sauce, and pumpkin pie. During grace, the smallest child reached out and swallowed the pill. Concerned parents made the mistake of giving him water, upon which he promptly exploded. Leacock says that when they finally pieced him together, there on his face was the contented look of a child who has just eaten a very large number of Christmas dinners.

Some Suggestions for Leading Grace Before Meals

A person leading the prayer before meals does not have to be a priest, deacon, or member of a religious order. This sharing of food at the main meal is a naturally holy time in the life of friends and family. Here are some suggestions for leading this prayer if you have decided to improvise:

1. Begin with a thanksgiving to God for the good things God has done for you.
2. Ask for a blessing on the food and those who prepared it.

3. Ask for a blessing on those who are present as well as loved ones who are absent.
4. Use simple and natural words. Pray to God as if you were talking to a friend.
5. Ask God's forgiveness for the wrongs you have done.
6. Pray for the world in its present needs.
7. Say a familiar prayer, but add to it specific prayer requests for what is happening at that particular time and place.
8. Create special graces that are suitable to the occasion, for Christmas, when there are guests, at a picnic, on birthdays, for the world's hungry, on Thanksgiving Day, for wedding celebrations, and so on.

You may also wish to consider a round-robin grace where each person at the table offers a thanksgiving for something received that day. Another idea is to create your own family blessing based on the words of the prayers in this book. Another option might be to sing the table prayer, making use of a favorite family hymn that is suitable to the season.

How to Use This Book

There are many ways in which the prayers in Part I can be used on a daily basis. The particular way may change from time to time, according to the specific circumstances. Ideally, one begins with an introduction, which normally should include the sign of the cross. After that comes a short responsory. Everyone present should participate by answering the response part. An optional Scripture reading is provided, though other suitable readings from appropriate sources may be used. This may be followed by the Lord's Prayer, which is probably the most ancient of table prayers that is said to this day by Christians of the East and West. The blessing then follows.

On a special feast or particular celebration one may begin the prayer with a hymn or refrain sung by all, thus honoring God with song and enriching the experience of all those present. If the group so chooses, they could pray the blessing together, though by nature this prayer is ordinarily said by one person in the name of all. At the end of the blessing, everyone present pronounces the *Amen*, thus giving their full assent to the prayer.

These prayers are not meant to be used only for groups or families. They are meant for both collective and individual use.

The thanksgiving prayer at the end of the meal is purposely kept short and simple. Examples of these may be found on pages 139–144 in Part II. These prayers are acknowledgments to God for gifts received. Again, this grace after meals may be said as a group or by one person alone.

The prayers in Part I should be used following the liturgical calendar and its particular seasons. There are four weeks of Ordinary Time which provide a month's variety before they begin to be repeated. For those who wish to honor the saints, there is a separate section of Part I in which their feasts and memorials are observed. The saints listed in this collection include those of the first ten centuries which belong to the common heritage of the one undivided Church. These saints are our fathers and mothers in the faith, who through the witness of their lives, contributed to the building up of the Body of Christ. Perhaps by honoring them we can work to rediscover our common roots and the unity which Christ wills for his Church. Some saints of the last ten centuries are also included, especially the great mystics such as Saint Teresa of Ávila, Saint Catherine of Genoa, and so on, whose writings enlighten us. There are also others, such as the humble Saint Bernadette, whose gospel way of life is a continual example for us all. In general, the saints presented are recognized by both Catholics and Orthodox, and are also honored by many Anglians, Lutherans, and other Christians. The examples of their lives and their teachings are a source of encouragement and strength for our common journey to God.

* * *

I wish to acknowledge gratefully some of the persons whose strong support made this work possible. First to Elise Boulding, who encouraged me almost twenty yours ago to compile the table prayers in use at Our Lady of the Resurrection monastery. Next, to Liguori Publications, in particular to Judy Bauer, who shows great interest in the work from the very beginning and gave it her support and helpful suggestions.

As the psalmist says: "Let us bless the Lord at all times," especially at the table, for providing for our daily nourishment and all our other needs. With Saint Paul, "Let us abound in thanksgiving" for the gifts received.

BROTHER VICTOR-ANTOINE
AUGUST 15, 2002
SOLEMNITY OF THE ASSUMPTION OF OUR LADY

BLESSINGS OF THE TABLE

Part I

TABLE PRAYERS ACCORDING TO THE CHURCH YEAR

ADVENT

Advent: Week 1

Optional Reading: Romans 13:11–12

Leader: The time appointed has come,
          our salvation is near.

All: Rejoice, daughter of Zion, your king is coming
          to you, Alleluia!

Optional Lord's Prayer

Blessing: O Lord, Our God,
          help us to prepare for the coming of Christ,
          your Son.
          When he comes, may he find us
          eagerly awaiting him in joyful prayer.
          Send your blessing upon this table
          and all those who share in this meal.
          This we ask through Christ, our Lord. Amen.

Advent: Week 2

Optional Reading: Matthew 11:2–6

Leader: A voice cries out in the desert:
"Prepare the way of the Lord."

All: Make straight the paths for our God.

Optional Lord's Prayer

Blessing: Blessed be you, God of the ancient prophets,
for you have sent John the Baptist
to prepare the way for Christ.
Open our hearts to the joy of Christ's coming,
and may this meal be eaten
in imitation of the simple honey
and locusts of John the Baptist.
As we await with hope
the blessed coming
of our Savior,
our Lord Jesus Christ.
Amen.

Advent: Week 3

Optional Reading: John 1:19–23

Leader: Drop down dew, O heavens, from above,
and let the clouds rain down the just one.
All: Let the earth be opened,
and bloom forth the Savior.

Optional Lord's Prayer

Blessing: Lord, Jesus Christ, Son of David,
and radiant star of morning,
come and dispel the darkness of our night.
We cry for you with one voice:
Come, Lord Jesus, Come!
Look with mercy upon us who await your coming.
Give us our daily bread
and grant us the grace to share one day
in the eternal banquet of your kingdom. Amen.

Advent: Week 4

Optional Reading: Luke 1:39–45

Leader: Behold, the time of our salvation is at hand,
for the Virgin approaches to give birth to her Son.

All: Be glad and rejoice, O Bethlehem,
for from you the Lord shall shine forth as the
dawn.

Optional Lord's Prayer

Blessing: Blessed be you, Lord Jesus Christ,
you see the need we have of your saving help.
You come to visit us to heal all our wounds.
Grant your blessings on this food
prepared for our nourishment,
and may we find consolation
in your forthcoming visitation. Amen.

CHRISTMAS SEASON

Christmas Eve: December 24

Optional Reading: Matthew 1:18–21

Leader: Let us celebrate, O people, the pre-feast
of Christ's Nativity.
Behold the Virgin in whose womb a spiritual
paradise is planted.

All: If we eat of this garden, we shall live forever,
for Christ is coming to restore us.

Optional Lord's Prayer

Blessing: Come, Lord Jesus, do not delay,
give new courage to your people
who trust in your love.

As we prepare to receive you,
we ask you to bless this table
and the food we share.
Provide for the needs of others until that day
when we all shall feast at your eternal banquet.
Amen.

Christmas Day: December 25

Optional Reading: Luke 2:1–6

Leader: Today the angels sing on earth,
unto us a child is born, Alleluia!

All: A Son is given to us. Alleluia!

Optional Lord's Prayer

Blessing: God, our Father, we bless you.
You so loved the world
that you have sent your Son to us,
Jesus, the Word made flesh.
We thank you, Our Father,
for this festive meal
which brings all of us together in joy.
On this day when we celebrate
the birth of your Son,
God, our Father, we praise you for giving us Jesus,
the light that rises in the night
and dispels all darkness. Amen.

Feast of the Holy Family

Optional Reading: Luke 2:39–40

Leader: Our Savior, the dayspring from the east,
has visited us from on high. Alleluia!

All: And we who were in darkness and shadow
have found the truth,
for the Lord is born of a virgin. Alleluia!

Optional Lord's Prayer

Blessing: Blessed be you, O God,
for through the mystery of the Incarnation
Christ was born into a human family
who gives to the world the beautiful example
of a family united in respect and love.
Teach us the dignity and sanctity of human love,
deepen in us our appreciation
of the value of family life,
and help us to live in peace with all people.

Give us the grace
to share this meal
together as a symbol
of our thanksgiving to
you. We ask this
through Christ, our
Lord.
Amen.

Solemnity of Mary, the Mother of God: January 1

Optional Reading: Luke 1:26–33

Leader: All of creation rejoices
in you, O Mary,
full of grace.

All: God made your body
a throne and your womb
more spacious
than the heavens.
Pray for us,
O Mother of God.

Optional Lord's Prayer

Blessing: Eternal God, as we enter this new year of grace,
may we be kept safe by the unfailing protection
of the Mother of God who brought us
life and salvation.
Bless all those present around this table
and the food which we are about to eat.
Make us always mindful of those who have
little or no food to eat.
In your loving providence,
also answer their daily needs.
Through Christ, our Lord. Amen.

Epiphany:
Sunday After January 1

Optional Reading: Matthew 2:7–12

Leader: From the East came the Magi to Bethlehem
to adore the Lord;
Opening their treasures,
they offered precious gifts:

All: Gold to the great King, incense to the true God,
and myrrh as symbol of his burial.

Optional Lord's Prayer

Blessing: Mighty God, you made manifest the mystery of
your Word made flesh with the witness of a
blazing star. And seeing it, the Magi came from
afar and offered you gifts. Grant that the star of
your holiness may shine forever within our hearts,
and that we may find our treasure in offering you
our praise and thanksgiving. Amen.

Baptism of the Lord: Sunday After the Epiphany

Optional Reading: John 1:29–34

Leader: Today in the Jordan as the Lord was baptized, the heavens opened and the voice of the Father was heard.

All: "This is my beloved Son in whom I am well pleased."

Optional Lord's Prayer

Blessing: Almighty, eternal God, when the Spirit descended upon Jesus at his baptism in the Jordan, you revealed him as your own beloved Son. Keep us, your children born of water and the Spirit, faithful to our calling.

Strengthen us with the nourishment of this meal which has been prepared by and for us, and keep us always safe under your loving protection, through Jesus your Son. Amen.

SEASON OF LENT

Ash Wednesday

Optional Reading: Matthew 6:16–18

Leader: Let us enter the season of Lent with joy,
cleansing our soul and body, limiting our food,
and striving to live by the virtues given to us
by the Holy Spirit.

All: This is the acceptable time to atone for our sins
and to seek our salvation.

Optional Lord's Prayer

Blessing: Lord, our God, we welcome the arrival of the
Lenten season. Allow us to follow the observance
of Lent with humble and contrite hearts. Bless our
daily nourishment, and inspire us to share our
food with the poor and the hungry. We ask you
this through Christ, our Lord. Amen.

Lent: Week 1

Optional Reading: Matthew 4:1–11

Leader: As we step into the holy season of Lent,
let us see as our destination the joy of Easter.
The journey may be long, but a radiant dawn
shines on the far horizon.

All: O God, Lover of humankind,
do not deprive us of our hope and expectation.

Optional Lord's Prayer

Blessing: God of love and tenderness, accept the prayers
and sacrifices we offer you as we undertake our
observance of Lent. May our fasting and prayer
increase in us a hunger for a deeper sharing in
Christ's death and Resurrection. Bless the food and
drink of your servants, that we may be renewed
and strengthened as we journey toward the joy
of Easter. Grant this through Christ, our Lord.
Amen.

Lent: Week 2

Optional Reading: Matthew 20:17–19

Leader: Let us fast, O faithful, from sin and corruption,
that we may receive a new life from the
cross of Christ.

All: Let us distribute bread to the hungry,
and welcome into our homes those who have no
roof over their heads, so that on completing our
Lenten journey we may receive great mercy
from Christ, our God.

Optional Lord's Prayer

Blessing: Almighty God, may these holy days of Lent serve
to enlighten us and help us grow inwardly closer
to you, while outwardly we grow closer to our
brothers and sisters in need. Bless this table, our
food, and those who have prepared it, and keep us
in good cheer during our pilgrimage toward the
Feast of feasts. Grant this through Christ, our
Lord. Amen.

Lent: Week 3

Optional Reading: Luke 16:19–25

Leader: Lent recalls Israel's forty years of wandering in the wilderness, during which the Chosen People left the captivity of Egypt, and crossed the Red Sea in search for the Promised Land.

All: There they received their earthly food from God in the form of manna from heaven.

Optional Lord's Prayer

Blessing: We bless you, Almighty God, and we give praise to your holy name. As we continue our Lenten journey, we ask your blessing on this food and drink at our table, that we may be properly renewed in body and spirit,

as we walk forward towards the joy of the feast of your salvation. We ask this in Jesus' name. Amen.

Lent: Week 4

Optional Reading: John 2:13–22

Leader: Lent recalls the forty days that the Lord Jesus spent in the desert, fighting against Satan, the tempter.

Let us remember the words of our Lord: "Worship the Lord your God, and serve only him" (Lk 4:8).

All: We cannot live on bread alone but by every word that comes from the mouth of God.

Optional Lord's Prayer

Blessing: Lord Jesus Christ, you have shown us that the desert is a place for meeting God. Help us to follow you into the desert land, there to fast, pray, and learn anew that the false values of self-indulgence and success can only lead to death and despair, and that our only hope lies in the paradox of the cross. Bless this food and those who share it together in your name. May we all be led to the fullness of life in your kingdom. Amen.

Lent: Week 5

Optional Reading: Luke 7:11–16

Leader: Let us slow down on the diversions of life and
return to God who gives us his love.

All: May we be faithful to the gospel,
for the kingdom of God is at hand.

Optional Lord's Prayer

Blessing: Lord Jesus, you teach us during these Lenten days
to apply ourselves to prayer and abstain from sin.
Help us during this blessed time to turn away
from evil so that we may worthily enter into the
mystery of your Passion and sing your praises on
Easter day. Send your blessings upon this table,
and upon all those who gather around it. May we
all be led to the glory of your kingdom. Amen.

Passion Sunday

Optional Reading: Mark 15:21–37

Leader: Rejoice and be glad, O church of God,
for your King comes seated in righteousness.

All: He comes seated on a donkey,
and the people sing: Hosanna in the highest!

Optional Lord's Prayer

Blessing: Blessed are you,
Lord our God,
in your only begotten Son, our Lord Jesus Christ.
In his infinite love for humanity he enters today
the city of Jerusalem, to undergo the sufferings
of his Passion, and thus reconcile our lost
humanity with you. Grant us to eat this meal
in the spirit of the
last meals of Jesus
with his disciples,
in true fellowship and
thanksgiving for your
mercy, and for all
that you have done
to save us. We ask
you this in the name
of the same Jesus,
our Lord. Amen.

PASCHAL TRIDUUM

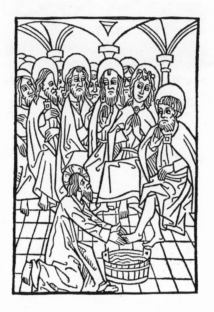

Holy Thursday

Optional Reading: John 13:1–9

Leader: Come, O faithful,
let us enjoy the master's hospitality,

All: and partake at the table of immortal life
in the upper room.

Optional Lord's Prayer

Blessing: Lord Jesus Christ, in your deep love for your
apostles you desired to share the Passover meal
with them on the night before you suffered.

During the course of that meal, you instituted the
sacrament of the Eucharist where you offered to
us your own body and blood as bread and wine to
nourish our souls. Send your blessings upon this
table and all who share this meal. Nourish us with
the Bread of Life, until the day we are called to be
with you in heaven. Amen.

Good Friday

Optional Reading: Psalm 21

Leader: You were led as a sheep to the slaughter,
O Christ, our God and King.

All: As an innocent Lamb, you were nailed
to the cross for our sins.

Optional Lord's Prayer

Blessing: Blessed are you, merciful Father. You sent to the
world your beloved Son, the Lamb of God,
to endure the sufferings of the cross and thus
accomplish the redemption of your people.
Grant through his passion and cross that we be
delivered from darkness and all evil.
Bless our nourishment on this day that it may give
us strength to continue our journey toward
the glory of Easter. We ask this in Jesus' name.
Amen.

Holy Saturday

Optional Reading: Jonah 3:1–10

Leader: O happy tomb! You received within yourself
the Creator and the Author of life.

All: O strange wonder! He who dwells on high
is sealed beneath the earth with his own consent.

Optional Lord's Prayer

Blessing: Blessed are you, God of the living and the dead,
today Jesus, your beloved Son, rests in the tomb,
having accomplished the work of our salvation.
From his tomb, new life is being offered to the
world, and both the living and the dead wait
in expectation of the glad tidings of the
Resurrection. Bless our food and our drink this
day, and prepare us through this nourishment

for the joys
of the Paschal
feast. We ask
this in Jesus'
name. Amen.

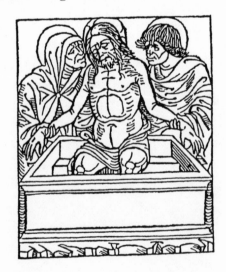

EASTER SEASON

Easter Sunday

Optional Reading: Mark 16:1–7

Leader: This is the day of the Lord's Resurrection.
Come, let us drink of the new water brought forth
from the fount of life springing from the tomb
of Christ.

All: Let us rejoice and offer a song of praise. Alleluia!

Optional Lord's Prayer

Blessing: Blessed are you, Lord Jesus, clothed in the
splendor of your Resurrection. You accepted death
on the cross for our sake, and the power of God

raised you up on the third day. Grant us the grace to celebrate this Easter festival with the new bread of sincerity and truth. Bless our Easter meal as you once blessed the meal with your disciples, and be forever present as a guest at our table until we join you in heaven. Amen.

Easter: Week 2

Optional Reading: Acts of the Apostles 13:26–33

Leader: Let us receive the glad tidings of Christ's Resurrection, saying:
"Rejoice and be glad, O Jerusalem.

All: For Christ has passed from death to Life, coming forth from the tomb like a triumphant bridegroom. Alleluia!

Optional Lord's Prayer

Blessing: Blessed are you, Lord Jesus Christ, the true Paschal Lamb, and the conqueror over death. After your Resurrection, you wished to share joyfully with your apostles, a simple meal of bread and fish. Bless the food and drink at this table, and make us sharers in the joy your disciples felt when they discovered your presence in the breaking of the bread. Amen.

Easter: Week 3

Optional Reading: John 10:11–16

Leader: On this feast of feasts we have been brought into the land overflowing with the milk of God's Word and the honey of the Eucharist.

All: This is the holy day on which we share in the new fruit of the vine and bless Christ forever.

Optional Lord's Prayer

Blessing: Praise to you, O God our father, who gives us the joy to share in the rising of Christ to new life. May the joy of our Paschal celebration remain with us all the days of our lives, and be a lasting sign of your loving presence among us. Bless our daily nourishment and all those present at this table. Make us always mindful of the needs of others. We ask you through Christ, our Risen Lord. Amen.

Easter: Week 4

Optional Reading: John 16:5–11

Leader: Our Lord's sheep will reach their grazing ground
where all will feed on the green pastures
of eternity.

All: Today all things are filled with light and joy.
Heaven and earth celebrate the Resurrection
of Christ. Alleluia!

Optional Lord's Prayer

Blessing: Lord Jesus Christ, on the evening of your
Resurrection, with eyes of faith, your disciples
recognized your presence during the breaking of
bread. Increase the gift of faith in all of us. May it
daily transform our lives, and allow us to discover
you anew in our brothers and sisters in need. Bless
this meal and those who share it with us. Keep us
always safe under the protection of your love.
Amen.

Easter: Week 5

Optional Reading: John 16:23–27

Leader: Let us celebrate this time of renewal,
this time of change, with a springtime
of our own spiritual rebirth.

All: Let sunlight overtake darkness,
and let truth abide with us forever. Alleluia!

Optional Lord's Prayer

Blessing: Blessed are you, eternal God, who makes us recall
during this blessed season the rising of Christ to
new life, the springtime of our redemption. By the
power of his Resurrection, grant us true renewal of
mind and body that we may walk in the steps of
the gospel with courage and strength. We thank
you for this meal, which comes to us from your
hand. May your blessing be upon it, and upon all
those who are gathered here with us. We ask this
in Jesus' name. Amen.

Easter: Week 6

Optional Reading: Luke 11:5–10

Leader: Since we have been raised to new life with Christ. Alleluia!

All: Let us seek the things from above. Alleluia!

Optional Lord's Prayer

Blessing: Eternal and merciful God, this celebration of the Easter mystery renews our covenant of friendship with you. May this new rebirth show its effects in the way we act and live.

Bless the food and drink at this table, and make us always mindful of the poor and hungry. We ask this through Christ, our risen Lord. Amen.

Ascension of the Lord

Optional Reading: Mark 16:14–20

Leader: O Lord, the angels
were amazed
at your ascension.

All: They were dazzled
as they beheld you
rising upon the clouds.

Optional Lord's Prayer

Blessing: O Lord, life-giving
Christ, after fulfilling
for us your plan of
redemption, from the
Mount of Olives you ascended in glory, in the
presence of your disciples. You are now enthroned
at the right hand of God, and from there you sent
to us the Holy Spirit, to enlighten, strengthen,
and save us. Send your blessing upon us and upon
this table today, as you sent it upon your disciples
before your departure, and may this food nourish
us for your service. Amen.

Easter: Week 7

Optional Reading: John 3:16–21

Leader: Christ ascended amid shouts of joy and trumpet blasts. Alleluia!

All: Today Christ is enthroned at the right hand of God the Father. Alleluia!

Optional Lord's Prayer

Blessing: Lord Jesus, Christ, our true God, you gloriously ascended into heaven, and gladdened the hearts of your disciples with the promise of the Holy Spirit. Send upon us also your life-giving Spirit, that he may heal us of our infirmities, confirm in us the faith, and console us in our affliction. Sanctify the food and drink at this table, multiply them in this room and throughout the world, and bring us all one day to the banquet of eternal life.

Pentecost

Optional Reading: Acts of the Apostles 2:1–12

Leader:　Heavenly Consoler and Spirit of Truth,
　　　　　you are present in all places and fill all things.

All:　　You are the treasury of blessings and giver of life;
　　　　　come, dwell in us and save our souls, O Holy
　　　　　One.

Optional Lord's Prayer

Blessing:　Come, Spirit of true light.
　　　　　Come, life eternal.
　　　　　Come, hidden mystery of God.
　　　　　Come, nameless treasure.
　　　　　Come, one who is beyond words.
　　　　　Come, source of all courage.
　　　　　Come, true hope of all the saved.
　　　　　Come, eternal joy.
　　　　　Come, my life and breath.
　　　　　Come, consolation of my soul.
　　　　　Come, O Spirit of truth, and bless the food and
　　　　　drink at this table, and grant that we may be
　　　　　nourished abundantly by the gift of your
　　　　　presence. Amen.

ORDINARY TIME
Feasts of the Lord

Trinity Sunday

Optional Reading: Luke 6:36–38

Leader: Blessed be the holy creator and ruler of all things,
All: The holy and undivided Trinity, now and forever.

Optional Lord's Prayer

Blessing: Almighty God, our help and our refuge, the
fountain of wisdom and tower of strength, you
know that we can do nothing without your
guidance and help. Direct us by your divine
wisdom so that we may live our Christian lives
faithfully and diligently according to your will,
that we may be profitable to ourselves and others
and to the glory of your holy name, for yours is
the glory of the Father, the Son, and the Holy
Spirit, now and forever. Amen.

Solemnity of the Body and Blood of Christ

Optional Reading: John 6:56–58

Leader: The wedding feast of the Lamb has begun. Alleluia!

All: And his bride is prepared to welcome him. Alleluia!

Optional Lord's Prayer

Blessing: Lord Jesus Christ, everlasting King, you who offered yourself to the Father upon the cross in atonement for the sins of the world, in this selfless act of love, you gave us your body for sacred food, and your most precious blood for life-giving drink. Make us worthy sharers in these mysteries.

Bless the food and drink at this table, that we may be properly renewed for your service. Amen.

Feast of the Sacred Heart of Jesus

Optional Reading: John 19:31–36

Leader: The Lord created us in his love,
and asks us to live in love and glorify him.

All: The Lord is our joy and gladness.
He is meek and gentle of heart.

Optional Lord's Prayer

Blessing: O Lord Jesus Christ, light everlasting, in your compassion you opened the eyes of the blind man, and offered refuge to sinners in the shelter of your divine heart. Open the eyes of our hearts to the mystery of your tender love for us. Bestow your blessing on this table and all those dear to us. Make us always mindful of the needs of our brothers and sisters. Amen.

Christ the King

Optional Reading: Roman 12:16–21

Leader: The reign of the Lord, our God Almighty, has begun.

All: Let us be glad and joyful and give glory to God.

Optional Lord's Prayer

Blessing: Lord Jesus Christ, eternal King and Giver of eternal life, look down with mercy on the weaknesses of our nature. Illumine us with the light of your divine knowledge. Shine forth in our darkened hearts, and make us eager for your kingdom. Bestow your blessing upon this table, as you blessed many times the table of your friends and disciples. Bring joy to all those who share this meal with us. Amen.

ORDINARY TIME

Sunday: Week 1

Optional Reading: 1 John 3:13–17

Leader: Make a joyful noise to the LORD, all the earth.
Worship the LORD with gladness.

All: Come into his presence with singing (Ps 100:1–2).

Optional Lord's Prayer

Blessing: O God, you dispel the darkness of our lives with
the shining glory of the resurrection of your Son.
Bless this food and drink which you provide for
us, that being renewed in body and soul, we may
serve you with the holiness of our lives. Amen.

Monday: Week 1

Optional Reading: John 15:1–5

Leader: Know that the Lord is God.
It is he that made us,
and we are his.

All: We are his people
and the sheep of his pasture.

Optional Lord's Prayer

Blessing: We bless you, O Lord, for your steadfast love
and for your wonderful works among us.
For you satisfy those who are thirsty,
and the hungry you fill with good things.
Glory to you, O Lord, for being the provider
of food for our bodies and the true nourishment
of our souls. Amen.

Tuesday: Week 1

Optional Reading: Luke 12:32–34

Leader: Enter his gates with thanksgiving,
and his courts with praise.

All: Give thanks to him, bless his name (Ps 100:4).

Optional Lord's Prayer

Blessing: Merciful God, you are great in compassion,
and your tenderness for us is without measure.
We ask you to give us today our daily bread,
and also to provide for the needs of all your
hungry children around the world. Through
Christ, your Son and our Lord. Amen.

Wednesday: Week I

Optional Reading: Matthew 25:1–13

Leader: For the LORD is good;
            His steadfast love endures forever,
All: and his faithfulness to all generations (Ps 100:5).

Optional Lord's Prayer

Blessing: Lord, Jesus Christ, we ask you to bless the food
              and drink set at this table. May they become the
              sign of your life in us, and may your love make us
              one. Amen.

Thursday: Week 1

Optional Reading: James 5:13–16

Leader: All your creatures look to you
All: to give them their food in due season (Ps 104:27).

Optional Lord's Prayer

Blessing: O you who clothe the lilies of the field
and feed the birds of the air,
who leads the sheep to pasture
and the hart to the water's side,
who has multiplied loaves and fishes
and converted water to wine,
do you come to our table
as giver and guest to dine.
Amen.

OLD ENGLISH TABLE PRAYER

Friday: Week I

Optional Reading: Matthew 18:1–5

Leader: The LORD is merciful and gracious,
All: Slow to anger and abounding in steadfast love (Ps 103:8).

Optional Lord's Prayer

Blessing: Blessed you be, O God our Father, in Jesus, your Son, who became human and died on the cross in order to lead us back to you. Grant us the grace to walk in the light of your love. Bless this food and drink of your servants, which we are about to

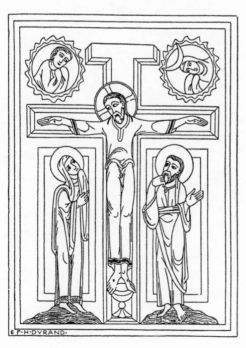

share in the name of the same Jesus, your Son. Amen.

Saturday: Week 1

Optional Reading: Proverbs 11:12–14

Leader: I find my delight in your commandments,
because I love them.

All: I revere your commandments, which I love,
and I will meditate on your statutes
(Ps 119:47–48).

Optional Lord's Prayer

Blessing: Father of mercies, in you is the source of life,
and in your light we see light. Strengthen us
with the nourishment of this meal,
and may Christ, your Son, dwell in our hearts
in love, both now and forever. Amen.

Sunday: Week 2

Optional Reading: Luke 11:27–28

Leader: This is the LORD's doing;
it is marvelous in our eyes.

All: This is the day that the LORD has made;
let us rejoice and be glad in it (Ps 118:23–24).

Optional Lord's Prayer

Blessing: We bless you, Lord our God, for through the
blood of your Son you have reconciled us with
you, and through his glorious resurrection you
have granted joy to the world. Bless our bread,
fruit of the earth and bless our drink, that both
may renew us in mind and body as we journey
toward the eternal
feast in your
kingdom, through
Christ, our Lord.
Amen.

Monday: Week 2

Optional Reading: Matthew 10:7–14

Leader: But know that the LORD has set apart
the faithful for himself;
the LORD hears when I call to him (Ps 4:3).

Optional Lord's Prayer

Blessing: O Eternal God, origin of divinity, good beyond
all that is good, fair beyond all that is fair, in
whom there is calmness, peace, and harmony:
make up for the dissensions which divide us from
each other and bring us back into the unity
of love, that to your divine nature we may bear
some resemblance. Bless the food and drink
of your servants, through the grace, the mercy,
and the tenderness of your only begotten Son,
Jesus the Christ, our Lord. Amen.

BASED ON A PRAYER BY DIONYSIUS OF ALEXANDRIA

Tuesday: Week 2

Optional Reading: Mark 7:31–36

Leader:　For you, O LORD,
　　　　have made me glad
　　　　by your work;
All:　At the works of your hands
　　　　I sing for joy
　　　　(Ps 92:4).

Optional Lord's Prayer

Blessing:　We pray and beseech you,
　　　　O good God and lover of humankind, to send
　　　　down to us the Paraclete, the Spirit of truth, holy,
　　　　and life-giving. He spoke in the law of old and by
　　　　the prophets and apostles. He is everywhere
　　　　present, and fills all things with joy. May your
　　　　Holy Spirit bless the food spread upon this table,
　　　　that we may be strengthened by it for your
　　　　service. And may he lead us all to the eternal
　　　　banquet of heaven. We ask this through Christ,
　　　　our Lord. Amen.

Wednesday: Week 2

Optional Reading: Luke 19:41–46

Leader: Unless the LORD builds the house,
those who build it labor in vain.

All: Unless the LORD guards the city,
the guard keeps watch in vain (Ps 127:1).

Optional Lord's Prayer

Blessing: Blessed be you God, our Maker, for you taught us
by the word and example of Christ, that we must
toil the land and work honorably in this world.
Grant us our daily nourishment of mind and body,
and provide also for the daily necessities of all

your children around
the world. We ask
you this through
Christ, our Lord.
Amen.

Thursday: Week 2

Optional Reading: Luke 5:1–10

Leader: Your word, O Lord, forever stands firm
in the heavens.

All: Your truth lasts from age to age,
like the earth you created.

Optional Lord's Prayer

Blessing: Lord God, by the power of your Word you made
heaven and earth and created all things. In the
fullness of time you sent your Son into the world,
the Word made flesh, to reconcile us with you,
and to teach us how to live in harmony as one
family. Bless our daily bread, and teach us that in
sharing this bread with those who are hungry, we
come closer to sharing in your divine life, which
you give us in Christ, your Son and our Lord.
Amen.

Friday: Week 2

Optional Reading: Matthew 11:28–29

Leader: It is good to give thanks to the LORD,
to sing praises to your name, O Most High;

All: To declare your steadfast love in the morning,
and your faithfulness by night (Ps 92:1–2).

Optional Lord's Prayer

Blessing: We bless you, O God, for the word and example
of Jesus, the Christ, who revealed your love to us
and instructed us to walk in the ways of love,
the most cherished of your commandments.
As we gather at this table to eat this meal we ask
you to bless our nourishment and to bring us one
day to love's eternal feast in your kingdom,
through Christ, our Lord. Amen.

Saturday: Week 2

Optional Reading: 1 Peter 3:8–12

Leader: Teach me your way, O LORD,
that I may walk in your truth.

All: Give me an undivided heart to revere your name
(Ps 86:11).

Optional Lord's Prayer

Blessing: Nourishing God, Creator of all good things,
you give us as food the fruits of the earth rendered
fruitful by the work of human hands. Bless this
meal and those who share it with us, and make us
always mindful of the work and suffering of those
who labor and toil on the land. We ask you
through Jesus, your Son and our Savior. Amen.

Sunday: Week 3

Optional Reading: Matthew 5:21–24

Leader: Christ loved us and poured out his blood
to free us from our sins.

All: By his actions he gave us a new life.
To him be glory and kingship forever.

Optional Lord's Prayer

Blessing: Lord God, source of all life, you grant joy and
peace to the world through the Resurrection of
your only begotten Son, our Lord Jesus Christ.
May he dwell forever in our hearts and through
the eating of this meal, may he grant strength and
renewal to our mortal bodies. We ask you this
through the same Christ, our Savior. Amen.

Our Father
in heaven...

Monday: Week 3

Optional Reading: Mark 8:1–9

Leader: Let us find gentleness
for it is a path to uncover the presence of God.

All: Learn from me for I am meek and gentle of heart,
says the Lord,
and you will find true rest for your souls.

Optional Lord's Prayer

Blessing: Generous God, you make yourself known to us
through the love of Christ, our humble and gentle
master. He teaches us to discover you anew in the
events of each day. Bless, O Lord, we pray, this
food and this drink which we receive from your
bounty, and may we enjoy forever the protection
of your love. Amen.

Tuesday: Week 3

Optional Reading: Matthew 7:15–20

Leader: Yahweh says: Act justly; rescue from the hands
of the oppressor anyone who has been wronged.
Do not ill-treat the stranger, the orphan,
the widow.

All: For the Lord is righteous and
he loves righteous deeds,
and the upright shall behold his face.

Optional Lord's Prayer

Blessing: Lord, our God, through the example of your only
Son, our Lord Jesus Christ, you encourage us to
walk the path of justice and peace, with special
concern and love for the poor, the oppressed, the
downtrodden. As we partake of this meal in your
presence, teach us to act to alleviate the hunger
and suffering of our brothers and sisters around
the world, through the same Jesus, your Son and
our Lord. Amen.

Wednesday: Week 3

Optional Reading: Luke 16:1–9

Leader: Let us approach the Lord in all openness
and simplicity.
Let us come to him in honesty and humility.

All: Good and upright is the Lord.
He leads the humble in what is right.

Optional Lord's Prayer

Blessing: Lord Jesus Christ, our God, you blessed the five
loaves and with them you fed thousands: do the
same, O Lord, with this food and drink. Multiply
them in this room and throughout the world.
Sanctity all the faithful who partake of them and
lead us all to eternal life. Amen.

Thursday: Week 3

Optional Reading: Luke 18:9–14

Leader: God's time offers us opportunities for grace,
All: So teach us to count our days that we may gain
a wise heart.

Optional Lord's Prayer

Blessing: Let us bless the Lord for his steadfast love and for
his wonderful works in our midst, for he satisfies
those who are thirsty, and the hungry he fills with
good things. Glory to you, O Christ the Lord,
the provider of food for our bodies and the true
nourishment of our souls. Amen.

Friday: Week 3

Optional Reading: Mark 7:31–36

Leader: Power belongs to God,
and steadfast love belongs to you, O Lord.

All: For you repay to all according to their works.

Optional Lord's Prayer

Blessing: Lord Jesus Christ, you are the true Bread of Life
that came down from heaven to feed all those
who are hungry for you. As we prepare to eat this
meal, we ask you to bless this food and this drink
which we receive from your hands. As you
provide for our needs today, help us to provide
for the needs of others. Amen.

Saturday: Week 3

Optional Reading: Luke 17:11–19

Leader: Bless the Lord, O my soul,

All: And all that is within me, bless his holy name.

Optional Lord's Prayer

Blessing: Stretch forth, O Lord, your helping hand from heaven, and bless the food and nourishment of your people. May all who partake of this meal be found worthy to share in the banquet of your heavenly kingdom. We ask you this through Christ, our Lord. Amen.

Sunday: Week 4

Optional Reading: Wisdom 16:20–21

Leader: We believe that, if we died with Christ, then we shall live with him too.

All: We know that Christ has been raised from the dead and will never die again. Death has no power over him any more.

Optional Lord's Prayer

Blessing: Your Resurrection, O Christ our Savior, has enlightened the whole world, and given new life to all creation. With the angels and archangels of heaven, today we sing and proclaim your Resurrection. As we praise you here on earth, make us worthy to eat of this meal with pure heart and pure mind, while we await your coming in glory. Amen.

Monday: Week 4

Optional Reading: Matthew 6:30–34

Leader: Our Lord's heart overflows with tenderness,
He is filled with deep compassion and patience.

All: The Lord delights in those who revere him,
in those who wait for his love.

Optional Lord's Prayer

Blessing: O Lord, bless this food, created by you, that it
may be a means of health to all. Grant by this
invocation of your holy name that all who share
this food may receive health of body and soul.
We ask you this through Christ, our Lord. Amen.

Tuesday: Week 4

Optional Reading: Luke 14:1–6

Leader: All is well with those who deal generously with
others, who conduct their affairs with justice.

All: Those who have distributed freely,
those who have given to the poor;
their righteousness endures forever.

Optional Lord's Prayer

Blessing: Father in heaven, through the words and example
of Jesus you show us your preference for the poor
and the needy. Teach us to share with them what
we have received from your abundance. Bless our
food and bless our drink, that being nourished by
them, we may serve you faithfully. We ask this
through Jesus, your Son. Amen.

Wednesday: Week 4

Optional Reading: Matthew 22:34–40

Leader: Bless the Lord, O my soul.
O Lord my God, you are very great.

All: You are clothed with honor and majesty,
wrapped in light as with a garment.

Optional Lord's Prayer

Blessing: Lord God, from your dwelling you water the hills;
earth drinks its fill of your gift. You make the grass
grow for the cattle and bring forth wheat from the
earth, the fruit of the vine to cheer our hearts,
oil to make our faces shine, and bread to
strengthen our hearts. Bless us, O Lord, and bless
this food which we eat together. Bless also those
who grew and
prepared it,
and give bread
to all those
who have
none. Amen.

Thursday: Week 4

Optional Reading: Ephesians 4:1–6

Leader:　The Lord provides seed for the sower
and food to eat.

All:　The Lord is my portion and my cup,
the delight of all my desires.

Optional Lord's Prayer

Blessing:　Lord God, we bless you for giving us your Word,
the Lord Jesus Christ, as a lamp to guide our steps
toward you, and as clear light for our path. Bless
this food and drink, also the food of our
neighbors, and give bread, peace, and joy to the
world. We ask you this in Jesus' name. Amen.

Friday: Week 4

Optional Reading: Micah 7:14–25

Leader: As a deer longs for flowing streams,
All: So my soul longs for you, O God.

Optional Lord's Prayer

Blessing: O Christ, our true God, bless the food and drink
of your servants, for you are holy always,
now and forever and ever. Amen.

Saturday: Week 4

Optional Reading: Luke 13:6–9

Leader: May his name endure forever,
    may his fame continue as long as the sun.

All: May all nations be blessed in him;
    may they pronounce him happy (Ps 72:17).

Optional Lord's Prayer

Blessing: God, our Father, teach us to live the gospel
    in a true spirit of joy, simplicity, mercy, and love
    for one another. We pray to you to bless the food
    and companionship shared at this table.
    We ask you this in Jesus' name. Amen.

SAINTS' DAYS

January 2:
Saint Basil the Great and
Saint Gregory Nazianzus

Optional Reading: Matthew 23:8–12

Leader: The bread that you store up belongs
to the hungry;
the garments that are unused
belong to the naked.

All: Take only according to your need,
and let the surplus to the needy.

Optional Lord's Prayer

Blessing: We bless you, Lord our God, for you enlighten the Church of the East and the West with the solid teachings of Saint Basil the Great and Saint Gregory Nazianzus. May we always be ready to live their teachings, as we seek to follow the path of the gospel shown to us by Christ, your Son. Bestow your blessing upon our food and make us not forget the needs of our brothers and sisters. Amen.

January 4:
Saint Elizabeth Ann Seton

Optional Reading: Sirach 3:17–24

Leader: May God defend the cause of the poor
All: And give deliverance to the needy.

Optional Lord's Prayer

Blessing: Fill our hearts, we ask you, O Lord, with love for you and unfailing charity for the poor as you did with the heart of Elizabeth Seton. We thank you for the dedication of her life to the poor and the needy, which you set as an example to all people. We thank you, also, for the fruits of the earth that you provide daily for our nourishment. May we always be ready to share them with those who have less than we do. Amen.

January 12:
Saint Aelred of Rievaulx, Abbot

Optional Reading: Matthew 5:14–16

Leader: Grant us, O Lord, the four qualities of a friend:
loyalty to friends in good times or bad;
discretion to know when to correct faults;

All: Patience to endure adversity on a friend's behalf;
and right intention to seek what is good
for the other.

Optional Lord's Prayer

Blessing: Pour into our hearts, O God, the Holy Spirit's gift
of love, that we, clasping each other's hand,
may share the joy of friendship, human and
divine, and with your servant Aelred draw many
to your community of love. Through the prayers
of Saint Aelred, bless this food and drink of your
servants that, being nourished by it, we may
persevere faithfully in your service. This we ask
through Christ, our Lord. Amen.

January 17:
Saint Antony the Great, Father of Monks

Optional Reading: Matthew 19:16–26

Leader: Holy Father Antony, you equaled Elijah in his zeal, and followed John the Baptist in his holy way of life.

All: You populated the wilderness with monks who were eager to follow in the footsteps of Christ.

Optional Lord's Prayer

Blessing: We praise you, merciful God, on this day in which we celebrate the memory of Saint Antony. Upon hearing the words of the gospel, Saint Antony accepted Christ's invitation to leave all things behind in order to follow him, and as a true inheritor of the fire of Pentecost, he led many to fullness of life in the Holy Spirit. We give you thanks, O Lord, for the wonders which you accomplished in Saint Antony. May his intercession make us ever aware of your gifts, including the food on our table, which we daily receive from your bounty. We ask you this through Christ, our Lord. Amen.

January 21:
Saint Agnes, Virgin and Martyr

Optional Reading: Matthew 13:44–46

Leader: Let us keep the feast of Saint Agnes,
by recalling her faith and suffering.

All: By the grace of God she overcame death
and entered into the fullness of eternal life.

Optional Lord's Prayer

Blessing: Almighty Lord, eternal God, you alone are the
all-merciful one. Look down upon us with great
mercy as we celebrate the birth of Saint Agnes

into eternal life. May the power
of her example inspire us to seek
your face with humble faith and
trust. Bless the food and drink
at this table, for you are blessed
forever and ever. Amen.

January 24:
Saint Francis de Sales, Bishop

Optional Reading: Ephesians 3:8–12

Leader: Happy are those whose hearts
are drawn into prayer.

All: In delight, may they meditate both day and night.

Optional Lord's Prayer

Blessing: We praise your holy name, O Lord, our God, for
by the example of Saint Francis de Sales you
remind us that we must practice constant prayer,
humility, meekness, and service to others. Bless
the food and drink present here on this table, may
this nourishment give us strength to walk in the
steps of the gospel. Amen.

January 25:
Conversion of Saint Paul

Optional Reading: Mark 16:15–18

Leader: You are a chosen instrument, holy apostle Paul.

All: You are a vessel of God's grace,
A preacher of truth to the whole world.

Optional Lord's Prayer

Blessing: O Lord, our God, through the teaching of your apostle Paul, you have made the light of the gospel shine throughout the world. We thank you for his conversion, and we ask you to give us the grace to follow his teaching. As we gather around this table, we ask your blessing on our food and on all of your sons and daughters. Amen.

February 2:
Presentation of the Lord in the Temple

Optional Reading: Luke 2:22–32

Leader: We magnify you, O Christ, Giver of life, whose mother brought you to the just elder, Simeon, in the holy temple in Jerusalem.

All: Receiving you in his arms, Simeon cried aloud: "Now, O Lord, let your servant depart in peace, for my eyes have seen your salvation."

Optional Lord's Prayer

Blessing: Lord, our God, today Christ, your only begotten Son, is carried into the temple in the arms of his mother where he is shown to the people of Israel to whom he brings salvation. Open our hearts to receive him that we may be enlightened by his presence, and sanctified by his visitation. Send your blessing upon this meal which we joyfully share in the same friendship we have with Jesus, your divine Son. Amen.

February 5:
Saint Agatha, Virgin and Martyr

Optional Reading: Luke 9:23–26

Leader: Agatha, joyful and enveloped in light,
walked to embrace martyrdom saying:

All: Lead me, Lord Jesus, to your eternal glory.

Optional Lord's Prayer

Blessing: Blessed be you, Lord God. You are the strength
of the martyrs and virgins whom you clothe with
your beauty. May the intercession of Saint
Agatha, who steadfastly kept the faith until death,
make us worthy to receive your pardon and
mercy. Bless our daily bread and drink and do not
let us forget the needs of those who are poor and
hungry. Through Christ, our Lord. Amen.

February 10:
Saint Scholastica, Nun

Optional Reading: Song of Songs 8:6–7

Leader: Let us rejoice in the merits of the gracious virgin,
         Scholastica, sister of Saint Benedict,

All: Who poured forth her tears
         of entreaty to the Lord,
         and was given much because of her great love.

Optional Lord's Prayer

Blessing: We praise your name, Lord and God, for you
         clothe the nun Scholastica with the virtue of
         innocence. During the course of a meal with her
         brother Benedict, she wished to celebrate your
         praises with him, and you granted her heart's
         desire. Grant us also the joy to proclaim your

praise as we share this
nourishment which
you lovingly provide
for us. We ask you this,
through Jesus,
your Son. Amen.

73

April 16:
Saint Bernadette Soubirous, Religious

Optional Reading: John 2:1–11

Leader: She is the wise and prudent virgin
whom the Lord found watching in prayer.

All: Saint Bernadette, pray for us to Christ, the Lord.

Optional Lord's Prayer

Blessing: Glory be to you, Lord our God. You are the
protector of the poor and the defense of the meek
and humble. In your mercy, you filled Saint
Bernadette with the virtues of patience and
charity, so that in all things she might imitate
the life of Christ. Through her prayerful
intercession, we ask you to bless our daily
nourishment that we may be properly renewed
for your service. Amen.

February 22:
Chair of Saint Peter, Apostle

Optional Reading: Matthew 16:13–19

Leader: Jesus asked Peter: "Simon, son of John,
            do you love me more than these others do?"

All: And Peter replied, "Lord, you know everything;
            you know that I love you."

Optional Lord's Prayer

Blessing: Lord Jesus Christ, you have built your church
            on the faith of Peter and the apostles. Grant us,
            through their intercession, to grow daily in faith

and a deeper love of you.
Bless this meal which is set
before us as you blessed
many times the meals
of your disciples.
Amen.

February 23:
Saint Polycarp, Bishop and Martyr

Optional Reading: John 15:18–21

Leader: I bless you, Lord God, because you have thought
me, Polycarp, worthy of this day and hour,

All: That I should have a share among the number
of martyrs in the cup of your Christ.

Optional Lord's Prayer

Blessing: God, our Father, you strengthened Saint Polycarp
and asked him to share in the company
of martyrs. Through his intercession, we ask you
to bless this meal and those who share it with us
that we may serve you faithfully all the days
of our lives. Amen.

March 7:
Saints Perpetua and Felicity, Martyrs

Optional Reading: Romans 8:31–39

Leader: The martyrs Perpetua and Felicity have washed
their robes in the blood of the Lamb.

All: And they were crowned
with glory and honor by the Lord.

Optional Lord's Prayer

Blessing: Almighty Lord, eternal God, today we honor the
virtuous lives and glorious martyrdom of your
saints, Perpetua and Felicity. May the example

of their lives encourage us
to greater fidelity in your
service. Bestow your blessing
on this food, we pray,
and on your sons and
daughters around the world.
We ask this through Jesus
Christ, your Son. Amen.

March 17:
Saint Patrick, Bishop and Monk

Optional Reading: 1 Peter 4:7–11

Leader: Blessed and wise Saint Patrick,
you received your call from God
to bring the faith to the people of Ireland.

All: And because of your obedience,
you were granted the gift of miracles
and of healing diseases.

Optional Lord's Prayer

Blessing: Grant us, Lord our God, the grace to follow
the example of Saint Patrick, not setting our
hearts on earthly things, but loving instead those
things that are heavenly. Bless our daily bread

and drink, and thus
strengthened anew,
may we serve you
faithfully. We ask you
this in Jesus' name.
Amen.

March 19:
Saint Joseph, Husband of Mary

Optional Reading: Matthew 1:18–25

Leader: O just and holy Joseph,
God has chosen you as the
foster father of his Son,
and the ever-virgin Mary was
entrusted to you as a bride.

All: Holy Joseph, you have
shown us the road to heaven.
Glory to the one who chose
you as the intercessor
for our souls.

Optional Lord's Prayer

Blessing: Blessed be you, God our
Father, for in your wisdom you chose Saint Joseph
to be the watchful servant who protected and
cared for the needs of Jesus and Mary. Grant us,
through his loving intercession, the grace to be
attentive to the needs of our brothers and sisters.
Bless the food and drink at our table, and renew us
in mind and body for your service. Through
Christ, our Lord. Amen.

March 25:
The Annunciation of the Lord

Optional Reading: Isaiah 7:14–16

Leader: The angel of the Lord brought
good tidings to Mary

All: And she conceived of the Holy Spirit.

Optional Lord's Prayer

Blessing: Today, a prelude of joy for the whole world, the
dawn of our salvation, is announced by Gabriel
to the Virgin Mary. Let us hasten to celebrate
with gladness, the coming of Christ among us,
the Christ who dwelt in the bosom of the Father
before time began. We pray, O Lord, as you once
came to dwell in Mary, you come today to live
among us, for you alone are the way, the truth,
and the life. Amen.

March 30:
Saint John Climacus, Abbot

Optional Reading: Isaiah 52:7–10

Leader: The Lord led you to the desert to be a guiding star, to Him be glory forever.

All: You show us by your example and teaching the way to heaven, O holy father and teacher John.

Optional Lord's Prayer

Blessing: We thank you, God of love, and we praise your holy name, for the example and teaching of John Climacus. For your sake he abandoned the false pleasures of the world and retired to the Sinai desert to follow Christ through fasting, watchfulness, and prayer. He practiced special love for the poor, and the sick he healed in your name. Bless, O Lord, the food and drink of your servants, may it renew our strength to follow you to the end. We ask you this through Christ, your Son. Amen.

April 2:
Saint Mary of Egypt, Hermitess

Optional Reading: Philippians 3:7–10

Leader: With eagerness and love, O Mary, you ran toward Christ, thus abandoning your former way of sin.

All: And being nourished in the untrodden wilderness, you chastely fulfilled his divine commandments.

Optional Lord's Prayer

Blessing: Blessed be you, God our Father, for in Saint Mary the Egyptian, you gave us an example of true conversion from sin into light.

By the stream of her tears she brought forth fruits of repentance. By fasting and abstinence, she conquered bodily passions. By accepting the silence of the desert and by constant prayer,

she choked the power of the evil one. Bless, O Lord, this meal we share, and grant that by following Mary of Egypt in the ways of repentance, we may come into the presence of Christ, your Son. Amen.

April 21:
Saint Anselm, Bishop and Doctor

Optional Reading: Ephesians 3:16–19

Leader: The saints will sing for joy in heaven's glory.

All: Radiant is their victory over human weakness.

Optional Lord's Prayer

Blessing: Praise be given to you, merciful God, for through the example and teaching of Saint Anselm you inspire us to follow Christ in our daily lives and work. By the intercession of his prayer, bless our food and drink which is provided by you to sustain us on our journey. Make us always grateful for all your gifts and ever mindful of the needs of others. Through Christ, our Lord. Amen.

April 29:
Saint Catherine of Siena, Virgin and Doctor

Optional Reading: Matthew 11:25–30

Leader: O God, food of the angels,
you give yourself to us.
You are beauty and
wisdom itself.

All: O Catherine, virgin of Christ,
Nothing can separate you
from the love of Christ.

Optional Lord's Prayer

Blessing: Compassionate God,
by the power of your
Holy Spirit you made your
dwelling place in the heart of the
pure virgin Catherine. Help us, through her
steadfast prayers, to remain worthy of your Spirit.
As we gather around this table,
we ask your blessing on our food and on all your
sons and daughters. We ask this in Jesus' name.
Amen.

May 1:
Saint Joseph the Worker

(See March 19.)

May 2:
Saint Athanasius, Bishop

Optional Reading: 1 John 5:1–5

Leader: Saint Athanasius proved himself
         a wise and faithful servant,
All: Therefore the Lord entrusted to him
         the care of his flock.

Optional Lord's Prayer

Blessing: Lord God, you called Saint Athanasius to be a defender of the faith, and a beacon of light to the Christian people. You made him a shepherd of the church so that the faithful may benefit from the wisdom and example of his life. Bless your flock, gathered around this table, and through the intercession of Saint Athanasius' prayers, grant that the nourishment of this meal may be ever beneficial to us. This we ask through Christ, our Lord. Amen.

May 15:
Saint Pachomius, Abbot

Optional Reading: Sirach 2:7–13

Leader: Your abundant tears made the desert
          sprout and bloom.

All: Holy Pachomius, pray to Christ to save our souls.

Optional Lord's Prayer

Blessing: Blessed be you, Lord God, on this day of
           celebrating the memory of the humble monk
           Pachomius. You inspired him to institute the
           monastic form of life as a way of following the
           gospel of Jesus Christ. Grant us, O God, by his
           intercession, to share this meal in the joy of the
           saints, keeping in mind the needs of the poor and
           the destitute. We ask this through Christ, our
           Lord. Amen.

May 25:
Saint Bede, the Venerable

Optional Reading: Luke 9:57–62

Leader: The person who obeys God's law
and teaches others to do so,

All: Will be great in the kingdom of heaven.

Optional Lord's Prayer

Blessing: We praise your name, merciful God, for you have
enlightened us, your children, with the teachings
of Saint Bede. With the help of his prayers, may
we grow daily in wisdom and in love of you. Send
your blessing upon this meal, which we are about
to share in Jesus' name. Amen.

May 31:
The Visitation

Optional Reading: Luke 1:39–45

Leader: Having begotten God in her womb,
the Virgin Mary hastened to Elizabeth.

All: Whose child understood this greeting
and who rejoiced with leapings and songs.

Optional Lord's Prayer

Blessing: Blessed be you, God of infinite tenderness,
for you inspired Mary, the humble maiden
of Nazareth, to visit her cousin Elizabeth and
to assist her in her human needs. Help us,
so that following
Mary's example,
we may remain always
open to the needs
of others. Fortify us
with the nourishment
of this meal, and bring
us one day to the
eternal feast in your
kingdom. Amen.

June 1:
Saint Justin, Martyr

Optional Reading: 1 Corinthians 1:18–23

Leader: "God's favor is stored up until the end," says Justin, "for all those who have lived good lives."

All: In all things let us praise the Creator through Jesus Christ, his Son, and the Holy Spirit.

Optional Lord's Prayer

Blessing: All praise be given to you, Lord Jesus, for the martyrdom of Saint Justin, who gave his life for you. Neither torture nor the fear of death could turn him away from his abiding faith in you. Through Saint Justin's intercession, bless our daily bread and drink which you have so generously provided for our needs. Amen.

June 9:
Saint Ephraem,
Monk, Deacon, and Doctor

Optional Reading: Colossians 3:15–17

Leader: My hunger takes delight in the fragrance
of paradise, for its scent gives nourishment
to me at all times.

All: Whoever inhales this sweetness is overjoyed,
and forgets his earthly bread.

Optional Lord's Prayer

Blessing: Blessed are you, God of Light, God of Love,
for you filled Saint Ephraem with the outpouring
of your Holy Spirit. Your Spirit inspired him to
serve you faithfully and to sing daily the praises
of your mysteries. As we gather around this table,
we ask your blessing on our food and drink.
May this meal be a sign of our unity with you
and all our sisters and brothers, we ask you this
through Christ, our Lord. Amen.

June 24:
Birth of John the Baptist

Optional Reading: Luke 1:5–25

Leader: Your glorious birth, O Holy Precursor,
All: Heralded the incarnation of the Son of God.

Optional Lord's Prayer

Blessing: May you be ever blessed, merciful God, for you
sent John the Baptist as forerunner, to prepare in
the desert a way for Christ, your Son. Open our
hearts to the power of his love, so that it may
steadily increase in us and daily transform our
lives. Through the prayers of John the Baptist,
may your blessing descend upon this table,
so that in partaking of this meal, we may continue
to praise you name forever. Amen.

June 28:
Saint Irenaeus, Bishop and Martyr

Optional Reading: 1 Timothy 2:22–26

Leader: Saint Irenaeus, true to his name,
made peace the object of his life,

All: And he labored to preserve
the unity of the Church.

Optional Lord's Prayer

Blessing: Almighty God, you inspired Saint Irenaeus to
teach your divine truth faithfully, and to preserve
the bond of unity in your Church. May we follow
his example, becoming ministers of peace and
reconciliation among all your people. Bestow your
blessing upon this food, and may we learn to share
it willingly with the poor, the hungry, and the
dispossessed. We ask this through Christ, our
Lord. Amen.

June 29:
Saints Peter and Paul, Apostles

Optional Reading: John 21:15–19

Leader: Rejoice, apostle Peter, so closely linked
with your teacher, Christ, our God.

All: Rejoice, O beloved Paul, preacher of the faith
and teacher to the gentiles.

Optional Lord's Prayer

Blessing: We praise your name, God almighty, as we keep
today a splendid festival, commemorating the
martyrdom of your glorious apostles, Peter and
Paul. By the merits of their prayers, strengthen us
in that faith which is built on the solid foundation
of the apostles. Bless the food and drink of your
servants. As we accept this food from your hand,
may we also receive your Word of life. Amen.

July 3:
Saint Thomas, Apostle

Optional Reading: John 20:24–29

Leader: Thomas, in touching the wounds of his Master's body, healed the wounds of our own disbelief.

All: Filled with divine grace, let us call out: "You are my Lord and my God."

Optional Lord's Prayer

Blessing: We bless you, God of all goodness, on this day of celebrating the feast of the apostle Thomas. May the example of his faith lead us to a firm belief in Christ as our Lord and God. Send your blessing upon this meal and on all who share it with us in the friendship we have in Jesus' name. Amen.

July 11:
Saint Benedict, Abbot

Optional Reading: Matthew 19:27–29

Leader: Let us practice good works and be guided by the gospel,

All: So that we my deserve to see him, who has called us to his kingdom.

Optional Lord's Prayer

Blessing: We bless your name, ever-faithful God, on this day as we keep the memory of our father in the faith, Saint Benedict. You made him a master and guide on the ways of monastic life, so that his disciples may tread the path of Christ. Through the help of his prayers, bless our daily food and drink, and grant that we may always love Christ above all else. Amen.

July 22:
Saint Mary Magdalene

Optional Reading: 2 Corinthians 5:14–17

Leader: How blessed you are, Mary Magdalene,
            apostle to the apostles,

All: For you were the first to proclaim
            that the Lord had truly risen.

Optional Lord's Prayer

Blessing: Holy and immortal God, we bless your name on
            this day honoring the life of your servant, Mary
            Magdalene. You chose her to be the first witness
            to the Resurrection of Christ, and sent her later
            to announce the good tidings to the disciples.
            May her prayers merit us to proclaim daily the

joyful news
of Christ's
Resurrection.
Bestow your
blessing on this
food, we pray,
and give us also
the Bread of
heaven that we
may have life
eternal. Amen.

July 26:
Saints Joachim and Anne, Parents of Mary

Optional Reading: Sirach 44:10–15

Leader: Joachim and Anne worshiped God
            day and night,
            waiting for the joy
            that is the honorable Virgin Mary,

All: The Mother of the Living God
            who comes to save his people.

Optional Lord's Prayer

Blessing: Ever-mighty Lord, God of our holy ancestors,
            you present the parenthood of Joachim and Ann
            as a model. You chose them to become the parents
            of Mary, and the glorious grandparents of your
            eternal Son. May their prayers grace our earthly
            meal here so that we may look forward in joyful
            anticipation to the heavenly banquet. Amen.

August 1:
Saint Alphonsus Liguori, Bishop and Founder

Optional Reading: Romans 8:1–4

Leader: God binds us to him with gifts of love,
giving us a soul made in his likeness,

All: And a body equipped with the senses, and an
overabundance of things of the earth for our use.

Optional Lord's Prayer

Blessing: You are blessed, Lord our God, for you introduce
again and again new examples of gospel living in
your Church. Today, as we keep memory of Saint
Alphonsus, we ask you to grant us the zeal for
souls which he possessed in so large a measure.
Bless our daily bread and drink, and all those
seated at this table. Lead us all to the joys of our
heavenly home. Amen.

August 4:
Saint John-Baptist Marie Vianney, Priest

Optional Reading: Ezekiel 3:17–19

Leader: Let us pray that our hearts are capable
of loving God.
Let us pray to taste of the sweetness of heaven.

All: May our sorrows melt away before our prayer,
like snow before the sun.

Optional Lord's Prayer

Blessing: Blessed be you, God of all goodness, for by the
exemplary life of John-Baptist Marie Vianney, you
encourage us to follow you and live the good
news of the gospel. John was a faithful priest-
servant, totally devoted to you and his flock.

May his example inspire us to bear in our lives the
fruits of true holiness. Bless the food and drink set
on this table. We thank you
for this your bountiful
provision. Amen.

August 6:
The Transfiguration

Optional Reading: Daniel 7:9–10

Leader: We magnify you, O Christ,
the giver of life and light
to our immortal souls.

All: We venerate your all-glorious
transfiguration when your glory
blazed upon your disciples.

Optional Lord's Prayer

Blessing: We praise your glory, God of all mercy, for you
have revealed to us the splendor of your divinity
in the transfigured face of Christ, your Son.

The light of Christ's
transfiguration fills the
world with joy. As happy
partakers of this joy today,
we ask you to bless our meal
which we receive
from your bounty.
Through Christ, our Lord.
Amen.

August 8:
Saint Dominic, Founder

Optional Reading: 1 Corinthians 2:1–9

Leader: Let us give our day to our
neighbor and our nights to God,

All: For we know that God assigns
his mercy to the day
and his song to the night.

Optional Lord's Prayer

Blessing: We praise your name, Lord our God,
today as we keep the memory
of Saint Dominic. He preached
the truth of the gospel, both by word and by the
example of his life. May his prayerful intercession
help us to hold fast to this truth in our daily lives.
Send your blessing upon this food which we are
about to share in the peace and joy of Christ, our
Lord. Amen.

August 10:
Saint Lawrence, Deacon and Martyr

Optional Reading: John 12:24–26

Leader: The holy and blessed Lawrence cried out:
"I worship my God and serve him alone."

All: Lawrence loved Christ in his life;
and in his death, he followed in his footsteps.

Optional Lord's Prayer

Blessing: Blessed be you, Lord God, for you made the
deacon Lawrence a model of dedication to the
poor and crowned his life with the glory of
martyrdom. Help us to follow his example and
always be attentive to the needs of our brothers
and sisters. Bless this meal that we share in your

presence; may it
nourish and
refresh us for
your service.
We ask this in
Jesus' name.
Amen.

August 11:
Saint Clare, Abbess

Optional Reading: Matthew 5:1–12

Leader: Love one another in the charity of Christ,
and call upon his mercy.

All: Let the love you have inwardly
be manifested outwardly by your works.

Optional Lord's Prayer

Blessing: Lord, almighty God, you called Saint Clare and
her companions to follow Christ, your Son, by
embracing a life of poverty and simplicity. Today,
as we celebrate her feast day, we ask you to grant
us the grace to imitate Clare's fidelity and
obedience to all the precepts of the Lord. Bless
our food and bless our drink, which we partake of
in the joy of knowing that all perfect gifts come
from you. Amen.

August 15:
The Assumption

Optional Reading: Revelation 11:1–6

Leader: Come, O peoples from all the ends of the earth,
let us praise Mary's glorious Assumption.

All: She has delivered her soul
into the hands of her Son,
and she bestows great mercy upon us.

Optional Lord's Prayer

Blessing: Almighty and eternal God, we give you thanks
for this day on which the Mother of your Son was
carried from earth to heaven. May she never cease
to intercede for us, obtaining peace and great

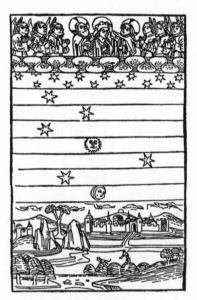

mercy for our world.
Grant us, O Lord, your
blessing on this food and
drink which we receive
from your bounty.
Amen.

August 20:
Saint Bernard of Clairvaux, Abbot

Optional Reading: John 17:1–11

Leader: Blessed Bernard, friend of Christ, the Bridegroom,
All: Your monastic life illumines us with the light
of true faith.

Optional Lord's Prayer

Blessing: Lord God, heavenly Father, today you fill your
people with joy as we celebrate the memory of
Saint Bernard, whose heart was filled with love
for you. May he obtain for us the grace of this
deep and steadfast love which is the sole reason
for our Christian lives. Glory to you, O Lord,

for being the provider
of food for our bodies
and the true nourishment
of our souls. Amen.

August 25:
Saint Louis, King of France

Optional Reading: Isaiah 58:6–9

Leader: Saint Louis said: "Be kind-hearted to the poor.
Give them as much help and consolation
as you can.

All: Thank God for all the benefits he has bestowed,
so that you may be worthy to receive greater."

Optional Lord's Prayer

Blessing: We glorify you, eternal God, for you raised Saint
Louis from the cares of earthly rule to the glory
of your heavenly kingdom. Through his

intercession, we ask you to
bless our daily food and drink,
and to not let us forget the
needs of those who are poor
and hungry. We ask you this
through Christ, our Lord.
Amen.

August 28:
Saint Augustine, Bishop

Optional Reading: 1 John 4:7–11

Leader: Let us say along with Saint Augustine: "I have tasted you, O God, and now I hunger and thirst for more."

All: "You touched me, and I burned for your peace."

Optional Lord's Prayer

Blessing: O Lord, almighty God, beauty ever ancient, yet ever new, you renew daily your Christian people by the power of the same Spirit who filled Saint Augustine with depths of wisdom and love. Through the power of the Holy Spirit, may we be renewed in body and soul by this food which you provide for our well-being. May we love you above all things all the days of our lives. We ask this through Jesus, your Son. Amen.

September 8:
The Birth of Mary

Optional Reading: Micah 5:2–5

Leader: Having brought into the world
the Mother of God,
Joachim and Anne rejoice.

All: With them we keep a holy festival today,
blessing the pure maiden,
born of the root of Jesse.

Optional Lord's Prayer

Blessing: Blessed be you, tender and loving Lord, for
through the birth of the Mother of God, you
announced to the world the good tidings of our
salvation. Mary is the true "bridge of life" who
contributes to our salvation by giving birth in time
to Christ, our Savior. By the intercession of her
prayers, we ask you to bless our daily bread and
drink, for our health and strength to do your work
depend on this nourishment. We ask this through
Jesus, Son of God and Son of Mary. Amen.

September 13:
Saint John Chrysostom, Bishop

Optional Reading: Ephesians 4:7–13

Leader: Holy John, grace shines forth from your mouth,
and like a torch it enlightens the universe.

All: He says: "Do not honor Christ
here in the Church in silken garments,
and neglect him outside
when he is cold and naked."

Optional Lord's Prayer

Blessing: Most holy and triune God,
you have given us in Saint
John Chrysostom a wise
teacher of the one God
in a Trinity of Persons.
We ask you to bless this
meal which we are about
to eat so that we may give
our lives to your service
more fully. Amen.

September 14:
Exaltation of the Holy Cross

Optional Reading: Philippians 2:6–11

Leader: As we behold the wood of the cross
            exalted on high today,

All: Let us glorify Christ who in his goodness
            was crucified upon it in the flesh.

Optional Lord's Prayer

Blessing: Lord Jesus Christ, by your suffering and death on
            the cross you make us aware of your immense love
            for us. May your holy cross be always a sign of
            your unfailing protection. Give us our daily bread
            that it may nourish us for your service. We ask this
            in your name. Amen.

September 15:
Saint Catherine of Genoa, Widow

Optional Reading: 1 Timothy 5:3–10

Leader: Let every moment of our lives be all in God,
whether we eat or drink, sleep or wake,

All: Whether we are in church or at home,
in good health or bad, at every day and hour.

Optional Lord's Prayer

Blessing: Lord, our God, we praise your holy name as we
celebrate the memory of your servant, Catherine
of Genoa. For your sake, she distributed her
earthly wealth to the poor, and wished to remain
united to Christ, your Son, in all things. Through
her prayers, we ask you to bless this food and
drink which we accept from your bounty. We
thank you for this gift and hope that we are
always worthy of your love. Amen.

September 17:
Saint Hildegard of Bingen, Abbess

Optional Reading: 1 Peter 4:7–11

Leader: O holy Hildegard, graced by the Holy Spirit,
you were commanded to write,

All: To tell the people of God
how to enter the kingdom of heaven.

Optional Lord's Prayer

Blessing: Almighty and eternal God, you made your grace
shine forth like fire from the lips of your servant
Hildegard in order to enlighten all creation.
By the power of the Holy Spirit she saw and heard
what others could not see or perceive. Guided by
her example and teaching, and nourished by this

meal which comes
from your hands,
lead us firmly on the
path of that kingdom
where Jesus is Lord,
forever and ever.
Amen.

September 21:
Saint Matthew, Apostle

Optional Reading: Matthew 9:9–13

Leader: Jesus saw a man named Matthew
sitting in the tax office.

All: He said to him, "Follow me."
And he got up and followed him.

Optional Lord's Prayer

Blessing: We praise your name, O Lord, God of mercy and
compassion, as we celebrate the life, the teaching,
and the martyrdom of your apostle Matthew who
left all things behind to follow you. Make us
strong in our resolve to follow you. Bless this meal
which we are about to share in the friendship
which we have in your name. Amen.

September 27:
Saint Vincent de Paul

Optional Reading: 1 Corinthians 1:26–31

Leader: Let us give mercy to others,
so that we meet no one in need without helping.

All: For what hope is there for us,
if God should withdraw his mercy from us?

Optional Lord's Prayer

Blessing: Be present at our table, Lord. Be everywhere
adored by your creatures. Grant that we may feast
here according to our bodily needs and feast in
paradise with you. Amen.

September 29:
Michael, Gabriel, and Raphael, Archangels

Optional Reading: Revelation 12:7–12

Leader: No evil shall befall you,
             no scourge shall come near your tent.
All: For he will command his angels
             to guard you in all your ways.

Optional Lord's Prayer

Blessing: Holy God, you have made the angels Michael,
              Gabriel, and Raphael to be servants of your glory
              and messengers of your faithful love for us.
              As they guide us with compassion and goodness,

may we become ever
more capable of
accomplishing the
tasks you give us to
do. Accept our thanks
for the food which
you have laid before us
and the watchful care
of your love.
Amen.

September 30:
Saint Jerome, Priest and Doctor

Optional Reading: 2 Timothy 3:14–17

Leader: Holy Jerome has said: "To be a Christian is the greatest thing, not just to seem one.

All: Somehow those who please the world the most are those who please Christ the least."

Optional Lord's Prayer

Blessing: We praise you, eternal God, for you filled our father in the faith, Saint Jerome, with the

Holy Spirit. Your Spirit gave him a taste for the study of sacred Scripture that he in turn used to instruct your people and enlighten the Church throughout the ages. Grant that we may be daily nourished by the wisdom of your Word, and the bread that you provide at this table. We ask you this through Christ, your Son. Amen.

October 1:
Saint Thérèse of the Child Jesus, Nun

Optional Reading: Hosea 2:14–15, 19–20

Leader: Truly I say to you, unless you change your lives
            and become like little children,

All: you will not enter the kingdom of heaven.

Optional Lord's Prayer

Blessing: We bless you, heavenly Father, on this feast of
            Saint Thérèse. For love of you, she was willing to
            become as a little child, allowing you to lead her
            through the ways of the gospel. Through her
            intercession, bless the food and drink at this table,
            and grant that we may be spiritually filled with
            the good things of your house. Through Christ,
            our Lord. Amen.

October 2:
The Guardian Angels

Optional Reading: Exodus 23:20–23

Leader: God gave his angels charge over us,
         to protect us in all our ways.

All: Along with our guardian angels,
         may we serve the Lord with love and devotion.

Optional Lord's Prayer

Blessing: Almighty God, our creator, we unite with the
         choir of angels to sing your praises daily. Today,
         we give you thanks for giving the angels to us,
         as messengers of your love and as protectors of
         our bodies and souls. Grant us to share this meal
         in peace, joy, and thanksgiving, being always
         aware of the unfailing protection of our guardian
         angels. We ask you this, through Christ,
         our Lord. Amen.

October 4:
Saint Francis of Assisi, Founder

Optional Reading: Galatians 6:14–18

Leader: Francis, while on earth, was a poor and lowly man.

All: Today he enters heaven rich in God's favor and is greeted with songs of rejoicing.

Optional Lord's Prayer

Blessing: Lord Jesus Christ, you gave us in Saint Francis a perfect example of humble gospel living. Today, as we celebrate the gift of his life, help us to walk in his footsteps in peace and joy, following the path your gospel has traced for us. Bless the food spread upon this table. Strengthen us by this nourishment that we may be lead to live in true holiness and simplicity of heart. Amen.

October 15:
Saint Teresa of Ávila, Nun and Foundress

Optional Reading: John 15:1–8

Leader: We need no wings to go in search of our God,
All: We need only to joyfully put all our trust in him.

Optional Lord's Prayer

Blessing: Blessed be you, God of our fathers and mothers,
for you filled the heart of Saint Teresa with zeal
for your service and an ardent love of souls.
Inspired by her holy teachings, grant us the grace
to walk daily in the way of perfection and
holiness. Thank you for this food and drink which
nourishes our bodies with the fruits of your gifts.
Amen.

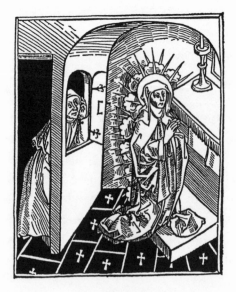

October 17:
Saint Ignatius of Antioch, Bishop and Martyr

Optional Reading: Philippians 3:17–21

Leader: Let us become God's wheat,
the pure bread of Christ.

All: Let us drink water with joy
from the spring of the Savior.

Optional Lord's Prayer

Blessing: All-powerful God, we praise your holy name for
the witness of the bishop and martyr, Ignatius of
Antioch. He offered himself as grain to be ground
by the teeth of the wild beasts, and thus presented
his life to you in sacrifice. Through Ignatius'
intercession, accept the humble tribute of our
lives, and grant that through the partaking of this
meal we may acquire greater sustenance to work
more faithful for your coming kingdom. Amen.

November 1:
All Saints

Optional Reading: Revelation 7:9–10

Leader: God himself is the eternal reward of all the saints;
All: Therefore let them praise and glorify God's name.

Optional Lord's Prayer

Blessing: Blessed are you, all-holy God, in the saintly men
and women of every time and place, who today
share in the glory of your kingdom. You knit them
together in a communion of love, in the
fellowship of the Church, which is the body
of Christ, your Son. Through the merits of their
prayerful intercession, may your blessing descend
on this meal and on those who share it with us.
Amen.

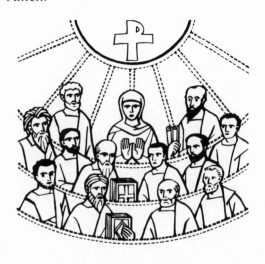

November 11:
Saint Martin of Tours, Monk and Bishop

Optional Reading: Matthew 25:31–36

Leader: Saint Martin loved God's people
and always prayed for them.

All: He spoke only of Christ, his peace and mercy
and his heart was filled with heavenly happiness.

Optional Lord's Prayer

Blessing: Lord God, source al all goodness, we praise you
on this day on which we celebrate the memory
of your faithful servant, Martin of Tours.
By the example of his life, renew in us the desire
to follow in the footsteps of Christ, your Son.
We thank you for this food which graces
our table, and we pray to you to bless it
so it may strengthen us for your service. Amen.

November 16:
Saint Gertrude the Great, Nun

Optional Reading: Psalm 23

Leader: The Lord loved holy Gertrude
with an everlasting love;
from her childhood, he drew her to himself.

All: Let us also follow the Lord,
practicing kindness and gentleness of heart.

Optional Lord's Prayer

Blessing: All praise to you, God of love and mercy, for you
poured your Holy Spirit into the heart of Saint
Gertrude and filled her with the delights of your
fatherly love. Today, on her feast day, we ask you
to pour out the Spirit into the emptiness of our
hearts, that we may learn to love you above all
things. Bestow your blessing on all who sit around
this table and upon our food, and make us always
mindful of the need of others. Through Christ,
our Lord. Amen.

November 21:
The Presentation of Mary

Optional Reading: Matthew 12:46–50

Leader: Mary is presented
by her parents
as an offering
in the temple.

All: We will rejoice
with her who is
to be the dwelling
place of the Lord.

Optional Lord's Prayer

Blessing: Blessed are you,
God of peace.
Today we celebrate the moment Mary entered
into the temple. There she is offered to you by
her parents and in turn she is fed by your divine
grace. Through her loving intercession,
we ask your blessing upon this table and upon
the nourishment we are about to consume.
May we always rejoice in the unfailing protection
of the Mother of God. Through Christ, our Lord.
Amen.

November 30:
Saint Andrew, Apostle

Optional Reading: Matthew 4:18–22

Leader: We praise the courage of Saint Andrew,
the "first-called" among the apostles and brother
of Peter, their leader,

All: For he is crying out to us:
"Come, we have found the one who
the world desires!"

Optional Lord's Prayer

Blessing: We praise you, Jesus Christ, for the faith of your
apostle Andrew, who as soon as he heard your
calling, left aside the nets which were his

livelihood and, without
hesitation, followed you.
May we be ever ready to
leave our worldly cares
and follow you at all times.
Bless our food and drink
as you many times blessed
the food and drink of your
apostles, for you alone are
all holy. Amen.

December 6:
Saint Nicholas, Bishop

Optional Reading: Luke 10:1–9

Leader: Holy Father Nicholas, your holiness of life
was set before your flock as a rule of faith.

All: You were a living example of meekness,
temperance, humility, and poverty of spirit.

Optional Lord's Prayer

Blessing: Almighty God, in your love for us, your children,
you inspired Bishop Nicholas to deeds of kindness
and relief for the poor. May the help of Nicholas's
prayers keep us safe from grief and danger, and
guide us on the path to our eternal salvation. Bless
us and these your gifts at our table, and grant that
through the breaking of bread together, we may
grow closer to you and to one another, in Jesus'
name. Amen.

December 8:
The Immaculate Conception

Optional Reading: Ephesians 1:3–10

Leader: Today the universe rejoices
for Anne has conceived the Mother of God,
in a manner beyond all telling.

All: Let us, then, glorify God at this wonderful
conception, for Mary is the city of God firmly
established on his holy mountain.

Optional Lord's Prayer

Blessing: Blessed are you, God all holy, as part of your plan
of salvation, you prepared the Virgin Mary to be
the mother of Jesus, by sanctifying her from the
time of conception. By the help of her prayers
may we be encouraged to lead lives of constant
fidelity as we await he who is to come. We give
you hearty thanks for the food and drink spread
before us. May it help us to do our work in
Christ's name. Amen.

December 14:
Saint John of the Cross,
Founder and Doctor

Optional Reading: Acts of the Apostles 13:26–33

Leader: Holy John of the Cross says:
"God is good and loves us with goodness,

All: God is wise and understanding and
loves us with gentleness."

Optional Lord's Prayer

Blessing: Compassionate God, you inspired your servant
John with a deep understanding for the mystery
of the cross and a fervent love for Jesus crucified.
Help us to follow in John's footsteps and carry our
daily cross without complaint, and thus one day
come to the light of your glory. We render you
thanks for this meal. May we feast not only on the
foods of the earth but also on the manna from
heaven. Amen.

December 26:
Saint Stephen, Martyr

Optional Reading: Acts of the Apostles 6:8–10, 7:54–58

Leader: As Stephen was being stoned,
             he could be heard praying:

All: "Lord Jesus, receive my spirit."

Optional Lord's Prayer

Blessing: Lord Jesus, you called Saint Stephen to
             discipleship to be the first martyr and witness
             of the early Christian community. Inspired by the
             example of his life, may we be moved to imitate
             his charity and to love our enemies for your sake.
             Bless the food spread upon this table. We ask that
             we may use the strength gained from it for your
             service. Amen.

December 27:
Saint John, Apostle and Evangelist

Optional Reading: 1 John 1:1–4

Leader: John said: "The revelation of God's love for us,
All: Is that God sent his only Son into the world."

Optional Lord's Prayer

Blessing: Lord, our God, your Holy Spirit filled the apostle
John with extraordinary light concerning your
mysteries, and with undying love for your only-
begotten Son. Open our hearts to the good news
he taught, and grant that we too may grow daily
in the love of our Lord Jesus Christ. Bless the food
and drink which you have provided for us so we
may cheerfully serve you in health and holiness.
Amen.

Part II

SHORTER
TABLE PRAYERS

BLESSINGS OF SPECIAL FOODS

A Prayer for the Blessings of Herbs

Almighty and everlasting God, by your word alone, you have made heaven and earth and all things visible and invisible. You have enriched the earth with plants and trees for the use of people and animals. You appointed each species to bring forth fruit of its own kind, not only to serve as food for living creatures but also as medicine for sick bodies.

With mind and body, we earnestly implore you in your goodness to bless these various herbs and add to their natural powers the healing power of your grace. May they keep off disease and adversity from the people and animals who use them in your name. We ask you this through our Lord Jesus Christ and the intercession of his holy mother and all the saints.

Blessing of Cheese and Eggs

O Lord, our God, the creator and maker of all things, bless this milk and these eggs; preserve them in your loving kindness for our use and nourishment as we partake of them. May we also be filled with your gifts, which you lavishly bestow in us with astounding goodness. For yours is the kingdom, and the power, and the glory of the Father, and of the Son, and of the Holy Spirit, now and forever. Amen.

Blessing of Grapes

Bless, O Lord, this new fruit of the vine, which you were pleased to bring to maturity through the passing of the seasons, the drops of the rain, and life-giving weather. Let this offspring of the vine be a source of joy for those who partake of it, and may we offer it to you for the cleansing of our sins. Through the sacred body and the holy blood of Christ, your Son, with whom you are blessed, together with the Holy Spirit, now and forever. Amen.

Blessing of Wine

Lord, Jesus Christ, by the pleadings of your most holy mother, you once blessed and multiplied the wine at the wedding feast of Cana, and at the end of your earthly life you chose to transform it into your most precious blood. Grant, we ask you, to bless and multiply the wine of this holy family or community and sanctify all those who drink of it. For you are blessed forever and ever. Amen.

Blessing of Oil

O God, sanctify this oil which you give for the health of those who use it. As you have anointed priests, prophets, and kings, grant that this oil likewise bestow strength and health on those who use it through Christ, our Lord. Amen.

Blessing of Drinking Water

Most merciful Lord, Jesus Christ, you once sanctified the waters by accepting to be baptized in the Jordan River. Grant, we beseech you, to bless and sanctify this water by sending upon it the cleansing power of your Holy Spirit. May this water be a fountain of healing for the souls and bodies of all those who drink of it and entreat God's protection upon themselves. Amen.

Blessing of Bread

O Lord, Jesus Christ, you are the bread of angels and the bread that gives eternal life. You came down from heaven for our sake and fed us with the spiritual food of your divine gifts. Look upon this bread, we humbly ask you, and as you once blessed the five loaves in the wilderness, so now also bless this bread and those who eat it. May this blessed bread be the source of bodily and spiritual health for all those who eat it, through the grace of your love for humankind. May it be for our sanctification and the nourishment of our bodies and souls. To you we give glory, together with the Father and the Holy Spirit, now and forever. Amen.

Blessing for the Fruits of the Earth

Father, creator of heaven and earth, you have beautified the sky with a crown of stars and illuminated it with the sun and the moon. You have also adorned the earth with its fruits to be of service and use to humankind. You have willed that all your people should rejoice in the bright shining of the sun and moon and be nourished by the fruits of the soil. Grant, we beseech you, to send us rains in abundance and to bless the earth with rich harvest and great fertility. We ask this of your goodness through your only-begotten Son, Jesus Christ, our Lord. Amen.

Blessing of the Olives

O Lord, by your word you have bid the earth to bring forth all kinds of fruits to refresh and feed humankind and all the beasts, we thank you for these first fruits which you have given us to enjoy. We praise you for all these gifts and for all the benefits which you bestow on us through you Son, Jesus Christ, our Lord. Amen.

Prayers of Thanksgiving After Meals

We thank you, O Christ, our God, for you have filled us with the good things of this earth. Deprive us not of the banquet in your heavenly kingdom, and as once you were present among your disciples, O Savior, and gave them peace, come also among us and save us. Amen.

BYZANTINE PRAYER

For this good food and joy renewed, we praise your name, O Lord.

A FRENCH THANKSGIVING

We thank you, Father, for the gifts of food and fellowship at this table, through Christ our Lord. Amen.

The blessing of God rest upon all those who have been kind to us, have cared for us, have worked for us, have served us, and have shared our bread with us at this table. Merciful God, reward all of them according to your promise. For yours is the kingdom, and the power, and the glory forever. Amen.

SAINT CYRIL OF ALEXANDRIA

Glory to you, O Lord, glory to you! We give you thanks for the food which you have given us in joy. Fill us also with your Holy Spirit and make us mindful of those who have less than we do. Amen.

Blessed be the Lord, the God of our ancestors, who is merciful to us, and nourishes us from his abundant goodness. Amen.

In peace let us pray to the Lord. Let each of us be mindful of all that we have received from his hands and for which we give thanks: food, family, friends, work, health, and happy memories. So, in giving thanks we are blessed. Amen.

TRADITIONAL CHRISTIAN PRAYER

O give thanks to the Lord, for he is good, for his love endures forever. He gives food to all flesh. O give thanks to the God of Heaven. Alleluia! Amen.

PSALM 136

Bless the Lord, O my soul, and all that is within me, bless his holy name. Bless the Lord, O my soul, and do not forget all his benefits. Amen.

PSALM 103

O servants of the Lord, praise his name. Blessed be the name of the Lord from this time on and forevermore. From the rising of the sun to its setting, the name of the Lord is to be praised. Amen.

PSALM 113

Praise God from whom all blessings flow.
Praise him, all creatures here below,
praise him above, O heavenly host,
praise Father, Son, and Holy Ghost. Amen.

You have filled us, O Lord, with your gifts.
As we thank you for your abundant goodness,
we ask you that this meal,
which was necessary for the strengthening of our bodies,
be also for the benefit of our souls. Amen.

ROMAN RITUAL

O God, our Father, we come to you at the close of this meal in thanksgiving, for you are the provider for our souls and bodies. Shine in the darkness of our night and forgive us our sins and failings. Through Christ, our Lord. Amen.

As we rise from this meal, may the blessing of God rest upon us, may his peace abide with us, may his presence illuminate our hearts now and forevermore. Amen.

Merciful God, we thank you for your gifts symbolized by the food we have eaten, and we ask you to give all people the food they need. May we all be united one day in the eternal singing of your praises, through Christ, our Lord. Amen.

To all else you have given us, O Lord, we ask for but one thing more: give us grateful hearts. Amen.

GEORGE HERBERT

We thank you, almighty God, for the food which we have received from your hands and for the gift of companionship at this table. Renewed by this nourishment of body and spirit, grant that we may continue our earthly pilgrimage in joy and peace until we arrive one day at the banquet feast of heaven. Amen.

May the abundance of this table never fail and never be less, thanks to the blessing of God, who has fed us and satisfied our needs. To him be all glory and honor forever. Amen.

<small>ARMENIAN PRAYER</small>

All-merciful God, you have fed us today from the abundance of your bounty. Fill us also with your compassion that we may walk in joy and thanksgiving all the days of our lives. Amen.

God is blessed in all his gifts and holy in all his works. May the name of the Lord be blessed now and forever. Amen.

Father in heaven, your tenderness is without measure, your compassion is without bounds. We thank you this day for our daily bread, and we ask you to provide for the needs of all your hungry children around the world. We ask you this through Christ, our Lord. Amen.

Dear Lord, we thank you for all the material and spiritual blessings that you have showered on us. Help us to share all that we have with those who are less fortunate. We ask this in Jesus' name. Amen.

KENT F. WARNER

Thank you for the world so sweet,
thank you for the food we eat,
thank you for the birds that sing,
thank you, God, for everything.
Amen.

E. RUTTER LEATHAM

Thank you, God, for the food received. Keep us ever humble, Lord, that we may be ready recipients of your goodness. Deliver us from pride and evil and supply the wants and needs of others. Amen.

ECUMENICAL AND INTERNATIONAL GRACES

May these words of praise ask you
for food for our offspring,
and for ourselves.
You are gracious to us.

THE HINDU UPANISHADS

Let us live happily, though we call nothing our own.
Let us be like God, feeding on love. Amen.

DHAMMAPADA

This meal is One.
This food is One.
We who offer this food are One.
The fire of hunger is also One.
All action is One.
We who understand this are One.

TRADITIONAL HINDU BLESSING BEFORE MEALS

O God, our Lord, cause a table
to descend unto us from heaven,
that the day of its descent may
become a festival day unto us;
and do you provide food for us,
for you are the best Provider.

THE KORAN

O Christ, our God, bless the
food and drink of your servants,
For you are holy always,
now and forever,
and unto ages of ages.
Amen.

TRADITIONAL ORTHODOX GRACE

Give me a good digestion, Lord,
and also something to digest;
Give me a healthy body, Lord,
and sense to keep it at its best;
Give me a healthy mind, good Lord,
to keep the good and pure in sight,
Which, seeing sin, is not appalled,
But finds a way to set it right.

Give me a mind that is not bound,
that does not whimper, whine, or sign.
Don't let me worry overmuch
about the fussy thing called "I."
Give me a sense of humor, Lord;
Give me the grace to see a joke,
To get some happiness from life
and pass it on to other folk.

THIS AGE-OLD PRAYER HAS BEEN FOUND ON THE WALL
OF ENGLAND'S CHESTER CATHEDRAL. IT HAS BEEN
ATTRIBUTED TO THOMAS H. B. WEBB.

May the blessing of the five
loaves and the two fishes
which God divided among
the Five Thousand be ours,
And may the King who made
the division put luck
in our food and in our portion.
Amen.

CELTIC MEAL PRAYER

Bless, O Lord, this food we are about to eat; and we pray to
you, O God, that it may be good for our body and soul;
and if there be any poor creature hungry or thirsty walking
along the road, send them into us that we can share this
food with them, just as you share your gifts with all of us.
Amen.

TRADITIONAL IRISH GRACE

Hail, hail, hail,
May happiness come.
May food come.
May corn come.
Just as the farmers work
And look forward to the reaping,
So may we sit again as we are sitting now.
May our enemies turn from us and go...
Lord, return among us and be our Guest.

GA OF GHANA

O God, thanks!
Today we bring you the food
that you have given us.
You, my termite heap on which I can lean,
from which come the termites that I eat;
Lord, we thank you; you have given us joy
with the numerous births you have given us.
Nothing of all that we offer you is worthy of you.

Pygmy of Zaire

We thank you, Heavenly Father,
For all things bright and good;
The seedtime and the harvest,
Our life, our health, our food.

German Prayer of Matthias Claudius (1740–1815)

Give us, Lord, a bit o' sun,
A bit o' work and a bit o' fun;
Give us all in the struggle and sputter
Our daily bread and a bit o' butter.
Give us health, our keep to make,
And a bit to spare for others' sake.
Amen.

Grace Written on the Wall of an Old English Inn

Almighty God, we lift up our hearts in gratitude to you, and
for all your loving-kindness, we bless your holy name:

- For life and health, for love and friendship, and for your
  goodness and mercy that have followed us all the days
  of our life;
- For the wonder and beauty of the world, and for all
  things true and honest, just and pure, lovely and
  of good report;

We praise you, O God, glory, thanksgiving,
and praise be unto You.

SCOTTISH GRACE

Christ, bread of life,
Come and bless this meal. Amen.
Cristo, pan de vida,
Ven y bendice esta comida. Amen.

SPANISH GRACE

Round the table
Peace and joy prevail.
May all who share
this meal's delight
enjoy countless more.

CHINESE TABLE BLESSING

For all your goodness and this meal,
receive, kind Lord, our thanks and praise. Amen.

SWEDISH TABLE PRAYER

Dear God, bless those who
bear the hardship of famine
and those who share their
plenty with others.
Wrap your love around those
who come to us in trust
and take care of those who
wander far from us in anger.
Amen.

HAWAIIAN MEAL BLESSING

Let us in peace eat the food
God has provided for us.
Praise be to God
for all his gifts.
Amen.

ARMENIAN GRACE

In the name of the Father, and of the Son, and of the Holy
Spirit. Let us eat, let us drink, acknowledging that all good
things come from God through Jesus Christ, our Savior.
Amen.

*Au nom du Père et du Fils et du Saint Esprit Mangeons, buvons,
reconnaisons que tous les biens viennent de Dieu, par Jesus Christ notre
Seigneur. Amen.*

FRENCH TABLE PRAYER

O Father, who feeds all that lives,
Crown our table with your blessing,
And feed and refresh us through the things
Obtained from your bountiful hand.
Teach us to guard ourselves from excess
So that we will behave as it should be.
Make us seek the things of heaven
And strengthen our souls through your Word
And Spirit. Amen.

DUTCH GRACE

Those who know that enough is enough will always have
enough. May we learn to be grateful for whatever we have
so that it may be enough.

LAO TZU

Table Blessings for Peace

O God of many names,
Lover of all nations.
We pray for peace
in our hearts,
in our homes,
in our communities,
in our nations,
and among nations,
in our world:
the peace of your will
the peace of our need.

Table Graces for Children

God is great, and God is good,
And we thank him for our food.
By his hand we all are fed.
Give us, Lord, our daily bread.
Amen.

Traditional Grace

God bless the master of this house.
God bless the mistress, too;
And all the little children
That round the table go.

Traditional English Blessing

For health and food,
For love and friends,
For everything
Thy goodness sends,
Father in heaven,
We thank thee.

RALPH WALDO EMERSON

Jesus, bless what you have given.
Feed our souls with bread from heaven.
Guide and lead us all the way,
In all that we may do and say.
Amen.

What God gives and what we take,
'Tis a gift for Christ, his sake;
Be the meal of beans or peas,
God be thanked for those and these;
Have we flesh, or have we fish,
All are fragments from his dish.

ROBERT HERRICK

The Lord is good to me,
And so I thank the Lord
For giving me the things I need,
The sun, the rain, the appleseed.
The Lord is good to me.

GRACE ATTRIBUTED TO JOHN CHAPMAN,
AMERICAN PLANTER OF APPLE TREES (1774–1845)

Meal time is here,
the board is spread.
Thanks be to God
Who gives us bread.
Amen.

TRADITIONAL

O Lord, your table here is spread
Which we are pleased to share;
We give you thanks for daily bread,
And for your love and care.
Amen.

TRADITIONAL

Dear Father, you have made us happy. Help us share our joy with others. We praise and thank you for our food. Amen.

We thank you, Lord, for happy hearts,
For rain and sunny weather.
We thank you, Lord, for this our food,
And that we are together. Amen.

Thank you, God
for milk and bread
and other good things
which we are fed.
Amen.

God bless us *(hands on head)*.
God bless this food *(hands around plate)*.
Amen *(hands folded)*.

Here a little child I stand
Heaving up my either hand;
Cold as paddocks* though they be,
Here I lift them up to thee,
For a benison** to fall
On our food and on us all.

   * toads
   ** benediction

ROBERT HERRICK

Thank you for the food we eat;
Thank you for the friends we meet;
Thank you for our work and play;
Thank you, God, for a happy day.

With heart as well as lips, dear God,
We thank you for this food;
For countless blessings too,
We offer gratitude.
Amen.

Before I take my pleasant food
I'll thank the Lord, who is so good
In sending all I need:
Now, Lord, be please, I entreat,
To bless this food that I may eat,
And be my constant friend.

A Child's Verse-Book of Devotion, 1840

TRADITIONAL TABLE PRAYERS

May the salt on this table remind us of the wisdom of our baptism, O Father. May the bread on this table remind us of the sacrifice of the altar. May the food remind us of your Word Incarnate. Amen.

Bless us, O Lord, and these thy gifts, which we are about to receive from thy bounty through Christ, our Lord. Amen.

TRADITIONAL CATHOLIC GRACE

Bless, O Christ, the social feast
    Here on our table spread,
By you alone let these be blessed,
    Each gift you do bestow,
And all are good, for they are Thine,
    And though are good, we know.
And you, O guests, I also ask
    To sing to Christ your praise,
And hymns of peace and saving grace
    Unto his honor raise.

ALCUIN, MONK OF CANTERBURY

Now we have both food and drink,
Our bodies to sustain;
Let us remember helpless folk,
Whom need does cause to sting.
And since our God is merciful,
Giving us such store;
So let us now be pitiful
In helping of the poor.
Then shall we find it true indeed
God will forsake us never,
But help us when we have most need,
To Whom be praise forever. Amen.

GEORGE BELLIN (1565)

159

O God who kindly does provide
    For every creature's want.
We bless you, God of nature wide,
    For all your goodness lent:
And if it please you, Heav'nly Guide,
    May never worse be sent:
But whether granted or denied,
    Lord, bless us with content.

ROBERT BURNS

As our bodies are sustained with this food,
May our hearts be nourished with true friendship
and our souls fed with truth. Amen.

O Lord,
As we are about to share the pleasures of this meal,
Bestow on us a hunger for holiness,
A thirst for truth,
A desire for justice,
A demand for peace.
Amen.

For food and drink and happy days,
Accept our gratitude and praise;
In serving others, Lord, may we
Repay in part our debt to thee.
Amen.

TRADITIONAL

At this table, Lord, we ask
    That you will be our guest.
We thank you, Father, for this food,
    And may we all be blessed.
Amen.

O God Provider, we thankfully acknowledge you as the
giver of all things that are necessary for the sustenance of
our bodies. Keep us always in your grace and love; redeem
us through your only Son, Jesus Christ, our Lord. Amen.

Dear Father of all mercies, we thank you for our daily
bread. Help us all each day to radiate more cheerfulness
and happiness. May we give more attention to the little
things of life. In thoughts, words, and deeds, help us to be
truly like you. In Christ's name. Amen.

Lord, we thank you for this place in which we dwell; for the
love that unites us; for the peace accorded us this day; for
the hope with which we expect on the morrow; for the
health, the work, the food, and the bright skies that make
our lives delightful; for our friends in all parts of the earth.
Amen.

ROBERT LOUIS STEVENSON

Our Father, we thank you that—
In back of the loaf is the snowy flour,
And in back of the flour is the mill,
And in back of the mill is the wheat and the shower,
And the sun and the Father's will. Amen.

TRADITIONAL

For the food we are about to eat,
Lord Jesus, make us grateful,
Bless the folks who helped to grow it,
And those who make it tasteful.
Amen.

For good food provided,
For good health to enjoy it,
For good friends to share it,
Thanks be to God.
Amen.

Brother and Lord, among your people sitting,
Lord of our toil, bestower of our rest,
Lord of our feast, to you as is most fitting,
Praises and thanks we bring, our whole heart's best.
Jesus, be our Guest.

THE ADELYNROOD GRACE

For what we are about to receive,
May the Lord make us truly grateful.
Amen.

God bless our fare,
God guide our ways,
God give us grace
Our Lord to please.
Amen.

Blessed are you, O Lord our God,
Eternal King, who feeds the whole world
With your goodness,
With grace, with loving kindness,
And with tender mercy.
Blessed are you, O Lord,
Who gives food to all.

<small>A Hebrew Blessing</small>

O God, bless this food
we are about to receive.
Give bread to those who hunger;
and hunger for justice to us
who have bread. Amen.

Lord, our God,
You have shown your love
by sending your Son
to eat with sinners.
Bless this meal,
and sanctify us
by his presence.
In the name of the Father,
and of the Son,
and of the Holy Spirit.
Amen.

M. D. BOUYER

Scriptural Passages
Often Used As Graces

Make a joyful noise to the Lord, all the earth.
Worship the Lord with gladness;
come into his presence with singing [...].
For the Lord is good;
his steadfast love endures forever,

PSALM 100:1, 5

Bless the LORD, O my soul,
    and all that is within me,
    bless his holy name [...]
    who crowns you with steadfast love and mercy,
who satisfies you with good as long as you live.

PSALM 103:1, 4–5

I will bless the LORD at all times;
    his praise shall continually be in my mouth [...].
The angel of the LORD encamps
    around those who fear him, and delivers them.
O taste and see that the LORD is good;
    happy are those who take refuge in him.

PSALM 34:1, 7–8

O give thanks to the LORD, for he is good;
    for his steadfast love endures forever [...].
Let [us] thank the LORD for his steadfast love,
    for his wonderful works to humankind.
For he satisfies the thirsty,
    and the hungry he fills with good things.

    PSALM 107:1, 8–9

I [...] go around your altar, O LORD,
singing aloud a song of thanksgiving.
    and telling all your wondrous deeds.
O LORD, I love the house in which you dwell,
    and the place where your glory abides.

    PSALM 26:6–8

Make me to know your ways, O LORD;
    teach me your paths.
Lead me in your truth, and teach me,
    for you are the God of my salvation;
    for you I wait all day long.
Be mindful of your mercy,
    O LORD, and of your steadfast love, [...]
Do not remember the sins of my youth.

    PSALM 25:4–7

I will recount the gracious deeds of the LORD,
    the praiseworthy acts of the LORD,
because of all that the LORD has done for us [...]
    according to the abundance of his steadfast love.

    ISAIAH 63:7

The LORD of hosts will protect them,
    and they shall devour and tread down the slingers;
they shall drink their blood like wine,
    and be full like a bowl. [...]
On that day the LORD their God will save them
    for they are the flock of his people;
for like the jewels of a crown
    they shall shine on his land.
God what goodness and beauty are his!
    Grain shall make the young men flourish,
    and new wine the young women.

    ZECHARIAH 9:15–17

The God who made the world and everything in it, he who
is Lord of heaven and earth, does not live in shrines made
by human hands, nor is he served by human hands, as
though he needed anything, since he himself gives to all
mortals life and breath and all things. From one ancestor he
made all nations to inhabit the whole earth, and he allotted
the times of their existence and the boundaries of the places
where they should live, so that they would search for God
and perhaps grope for him and find him—though indeed
he is not far from each one of us.

    ACTS 17:24–27

Blessed be the name of God from age to age,
   for wisdom and power are his.
He changes times and seasons,
   deposes kings and sets up kings;
he gives wisdom to the wise
   and knowledge to those who have understanding. [...]
To you, O God of my ancestors,
   I give thanks and praise,
for you have given me wisdom and power.

DANIEL 2:20–23

Let the peoples praise you, O God;
   let all the peoples praise you.
The earth has yielded its increase;
   God, our God, has blessed us.
May God continue to bless us;
   let all the ends of the earth revere him.

PSALM 67:5–7

All the days of the poor are hard,
   but a cheerful heart has a continual feast.
Better is a little with the fear of the LORD
   than a great treasure and trouble with it.
Better is a dinner of vegetables where love is
   than a fatted ox and hatred with it.

PROVERBS 15:15–17

Everything created by God is good, and nothing is to be rejected, provided it is received with thanksgiving, for it is sanctified by God's word and by prayer.

1 TIMOTHY 4:4–5

We brought nothing into the world, so that we can take nothing out of it; but if we have food and clothing, we will be content with these. But those who want to be rich fall into temptation and are trapped by many senseless and harmful desires that plunge people into ruin and destruction. […] As for those who in the present age are rich, command them not to be haughty, or to set their hopes on the uncertainty of riches, but rather on God who richly provides us everything for our enjoyment. They are to do good, to be rich in good works, generous, and ready to share, thus storing up for themselves the treasure of a good foundation for the future, so that they may take hold of the life that really is life.

1 TIMOTHY 6:6–9, 17–19

Blessed be the God and Father of our Lord Jesus Christ! By his great mercy he has given us a new birth into a living hope through the resurrection of Jesus Christ from the dead, and into an inheritance that is imperishable, undefiled, and unfading.

1 PETER 1:3–4

The one who sows sparingly will also reap sparingly, and the one who sows bountifully will also reap bountifully [...] for God loves a cheerful giver. And God is able to provide you with every blessing in abundance, so that by always having enough of everything, you may share abundantly in every good work. [...] He who supplies seed to the sower and bread for food will supply and multiply your seed for sowing and increase the harvest of your righteousness. You will be enriched in every way for your great generosity, which will produce thanksgiving to God.

2 CORINTHIANS 9:6–8, 10–11

Whether you eat or drink, or whatever you do, do everything for the glory of God.

1 CORINTHIANS 10:31

The LORD is my shepherd, I shall not want.
   He makes me lie down in green pastures;
he leads me beside still waters;
   he restores my soul.
He leads me in right paths
   for his name's sake.
Even though I walk through the darkest valley,
   I fear no evil;
for you are with me; […]
You prepare a table before me
   in the presence of my enemies;
you anoint my head with oil;
   my cup overflows.
Surely goodness and mercy shall follow me
   all the days of my life,
and I shall dwell in the house of the LORD.

PSALM 23